Mark J. Temmer

ART AND INFLUENCE OF JEAN-JACQUES ROUSSEAU: THE PASTORAL, GOETHE, GOTTFRIED KELLER, AND OTHER ESSAYS

CHAPEL HILL

THE UNIVERSITY OF NORTH CAROLINA PRESS

Library of Congress Catalogue Card Number: 73-8085
Temmer, Mark J
  Art and influence of Jean-Jacques Rousseau.
  PQ2057.A2T4   848'.5'09
  ISBN 0-8078-7056-0

Printed in the U.S.A. by Monotype Composition Co., Inc.
Baltimore, Maryland © Copyright 1973 in the U.S.A.

iv

à Henri Peyre
en témoignage de ma profonde
reconnaissance
et de mon admiration

ACKNOWLEDGMENTS

I should like to thank Professors
Stuart Atkins, Howard Clarke and
Jorge de Sena for their help and
encouragement, as well as Mrs. Ann
Pritchard-Kreyche and Mr. Donald
Fitch, reference librarians at the
University of California at Santa
Barbara

Chapter I was originally published in abbreviated form under the
title of "Art and Love in the *Confessions* of Jean-Jacques Rousseau" in *PMLA*, LXXIII, June 1958 and is reprinted by permis-
sion of the Modern Language Association of America. Chapter II
appeared under the same title in a shorter version as a contribution to *The Persistent Voice: Essays on Hellenism in French
Literature since the Eighteenth Century in honor of Henri Peyre*
(New York University Press, 1971). Chapter III was published in
Revue de littérature comparée, Avril–Juin, 1970, No. 2. Chapter IV
appeared as a contribution to a special issue on Rousseau in
Studies in Romanticism, X, 1971, No. 4. Chapter V was published
in abbreviated form in a special issue on Rousseau in *Yale French
Studies*, No. 28, 1961.

TABLE OF CONTENTS

"Love, Art, and Mme de Warens"

L'argile rouge a bu la blanche espèce,
Le don de vivre a passé dans les fleurs! (Valéry)

There are few men who have not despaired of settling the contro-
versies that relate to Jean-Jacques Rousseau. Well known during
his lifetime, these disputes have become legends which obscure the
real ambiguities of his existence and achievement. In this respect,
Rousseau belongs to the family of Montaigne and Gide, whose
lengthy confessions have rarely been judged in an unbiased manner. It is, to be sure, the very purpose of such avowals to preclude
indifference, and, in the case of Rousseau, there is little sense in
trying to evade the haunting and problematical implications of his
autobiography. It must be studied not only for itself, but also because the *Discours sur les arts et les sciences,* the *Discours sur
l'origine de l'inégalité,* the *Contrat Social,* the *Emile,* and *La
Nouvelle Héloïse* are transpositions of, and solutions to, Rousseau's
life. At present there is agreement on at least this one point, and
many philosophers and critics have sought to find the principle
which would reveal the true motives of a man who swore to tell
the truth. However, few of their commentaries on the *Confessions*
and the *Rêveries du promeneur solitaire* envisage the fundamental
question of the autobiographical genre itself, namely: *How does
the great autobiographer succeed in making credible and convincing the story of his life, and what are the stylistic means by
which he imposes this vision on others?*
    Indeed, the problem of verisimilitude has been generally
neglected. Rousseau's critics have preferred either to deal with the
man and to judge the uncertain values of his work, or to verify
the historical accuracy of the autobiography rather than to cast
light on the artistic metamorphosis of these data. The following
analysis is therefore presented with the intention of showing how
a seemingly sincere style and a moving appeal to the reader's sympathy made possible a self-recreation which reconciles art to life.

1

Sympathetic readers, it will be seen, should be especially wary of Jean-Jacques' disarming sincerity, which casts an imperceptible spell as they turn the pages of his book. The progressive crystallization of the artistic vision, this *mécanique de la vraisemblance* cannot be understood by the study of disconnected chapters and episodes. On the contrary, the captivation of the reader depends upon his willingness to accept the temporal perspective of the author, and, because of the stylistic importance of his suggestions of an illusory past, present, and future, I should like to focus attention on the nature of the sequence of his remarks about Mme de Warens. Everyone knows of her, for Jean-Jacques' first love is still a subject of scandal not only among the fanciers of *les vies romancées,* but even among theologians and moralists. It is especially the latter who have discovered a possible discrepancy between the beauty of her portrait and her true virtues. And it is precisely the tragic gap between *Dichtung* and *Wahrheit* which has caused them to question the story of the Charmettes which became an ideal of the romantic age.

It would, therefore, seem necessary to review the history of the Baronne de Warens. According to J. R. Benedetto she appears to have been quite ordinary: ". . . une âme commune, sans solidité ni distinction. Une imagination déréglée, accompagnée d'une sensibilité pauvre et d'une intelligence médiocre et au service d'un égoïsme un peu vulgaire, voilà en effet toute Mme de Warens. Sous l'extérieur agréable, aucun fond, aucun sérieux rien qu'un orgueil exagéré et qu'une versatilité effrayante . . . . une Bovary supérieure, plus robuste ou plus heureuse."[1] He then proceeds to disclose the truth about Jean-Jacques' youth, showing that Rousseau was only an apologist who distorted his history in conformity with his need for self-justification. Others, more indulgent, have defended the truth of the *Confessions:* so did Arsène Houssaye, whose book *Les Charmettes, Jean-Jacques Rousseau et Mme de Warens* has an elegiac charm which is still moving. Is it then possible that Rousseau wrote: ". . . . ce qu'on se doit à soi-même, ce qu'on doit à la vérité pour elle seule?" (IVe *Prom.,* I, p. 1028)[2] In raising this question it is not my purpose to doubt the value of past research, provided that it does not falsify the designs of the artist. "On ne corrige pas un chef-d'œuvre . . . ."[3] Jean Guéhenno wisely declares, and critics would do well to recall his admonition and to consider Rousseau's memories from the viewpoint of the writer. In this way, it may be possible to understand the surprising truth that the very arrangement of these recollections *is* the fabric of illusory time within the autobiography. This duration is real to the extent that Rousseau supposedly once lived these memories; it is illusory to the extent that the literary time of the *Confessions* is the result of a collaboration between Rousseau and his reader. The latter, whose psychology remains to be studied, is subtly guided by our author, who happens to be the only classical writer so familiar to us that we call him by his Christian name. Like Boswell, he needs to make friends and accomplices, knowing that in order "to show a man in all the truth of nature" he must above all superimpose a semblance of time or life upon the consciousness of his reading public. This ascendancy is achieved not only by quasi-mechanical means such as carefully prepared transitions, or even the relative length of the narrative (after all, reading Rousseau demands giving up weeks and years of one's life), but also by an artful control of the thoughts of the reader who is led to lend his own knowledge of time to strengthen the credibility of Jean-Jacques' self-recreation.

One may rest assured that the autobiographer took care not to present a careless juxtaposition of past incidents and feelings. On the contrary, to relate life is to simulate the characteristics of time as they are experienced, whether they are the uncertainty of things to come, the solidity of the present, or the redoubtable quiescence of what is past.

But how could this be done? In what manner did Rousseau create time and fabricate duration?[4] These are questions that can only be answered by the artist himself, and it is fortunate that he offers some hints which, however, pertain to music and not to literature:

L'imitation de la peinture est toujours froide parce qu'elle manque de cette succession d'idées et d'impressions qui échauffe l'âme par degrés, et que tout est dit au premier coup d'œil . . . Il [l'art] sait exciter par un sens des émotions semblables à celles qu'on peut exciter par un autre et, comme le rapport ne peut être sensible que l'impression ne soit forte, la peinture dénuée de cette force, rend difficilement à la musique les imitations que celle-ci tire d'elle. Que toute la nature soit endormie, celui qui la contemple ne dort pas; et l'art du musicien consiste à substituer à l'image insensible de l'objet celle des mouvements que sa présence excite dans l'esprit du spectateur; il ne représente pas directement la chose, mais il réveille dans notre âme le même sentiment qu'on éprouve en la voyant.[5]

The analogy is manifest; it is a question of suggesting gradually to the reader's mind an orderly succession of images drawn from a fund of experiences shared by all.

The first book of the *Confessions* is of fundamental importance, since it constitutes the basis of the aforesaid development. Almost imperceptibly, the reader enters Rousseau's past. This is achieved by virtue of a magnificent description of youth which is universally true for all men. In it, chronology is neglected and replaced by a calendar of feelings which tells of the development of the soul. Like Proust, Rousseau is forever preoccupied with childhood memories: "Dans tant de menus détails qui me charment et dont j'excéde souvent mon lecteur je mets pourtant une discretion dont il ne se douteroit guéres si je n'avois soin de l'en avertir" (I, 235). These recollections are put forth in this order: father, mother, feeling, libido, fellow men, theft, injustice, justice, books, apprenticeship, and departure. The meaning and sequence of such themes are easy to recognize; the mood is serene and seldom touched by melancholy which, were it too heavy, would destroy the universal appeal of his experiences. These reminiscences rise from the affective memory and are never deformed by intrusions of the mature mind. The latter serves solely to delineate the structure of the past, but does not project recollections into the artistic consciousness.

The transition between the first and second book is ingenious in that it foreshadows Jean-Jacques' meeting with Mme de Warens. Rousseau describes the runaway's frame of mind and recreates his ardent hopes for love and freedom. The vividness of these pages is the result of an interesting inversion in exposition. Before telling of his encounter with Mme de Warens, Rousseau dwells on the folly and vanity of his juvenile aspirations. But whereas most writers prefer to depict the idyll of youth which is then *followed* by disenchantment, Rousseau here reverses this customary order by first insisting at length on "the evils, the errors, the pitfalls and the enslavement" (I, 45, my trans.) of his life. This initial admission of deep suffering exhausts, as it were, the very reality of these sorrows. Thus, the reader becomes effectively the confessor who forgives and hence forgets. A new start is now possible and the psychological void in the reader's mind is then artfully filled with feelings of happiness and independence: "Libre et maitre de moi-même, je croyois pouvoir tout faire, atteindre à tout: je n'avois

qu'à m'élancer pour m'élever et voler dans les airs. J'entrois avec
sécurité dans le vaste espace du monde . . . (I, 45)."
Rousseau's presentation of Mme de Warens is both moving and
ironic: "Dieu vous appelle, me dit M. de Pontverre. Allez à
Annecy; vous y trouverez une bonne Dame bien charitable, que les
bienfaits du Roi mettent en état de retirer d'autres ames de
l'erreur dont elle est sortie elle-même" (I, 47). Here is the description of the meeting so well remembered by Stendhal and Balzac:
"Je ne trouvai point Made de Warens; on me dit qu'elle venoit de
sortir pour aller à l'Eglise. C'étoit le jour des Rameaux de l'année
1728. Je cours pour la suivre: je la vois, je l'atteins, je lui parle . . .
je dois me souvenir du lieu; je l'ai souvent depuis mouillé de mes
larmes et couvert de mes baisers" (I, 48, 9). The mood of introduction to happiness is grave and the solemnity of the occasion
stressed by the carillon of the Franciscan church—an unforgettable
day evoked once more on the last page ever written by Rousseau.
The past gives way suddenly to a present overflowing with desire:
"je la vois, je l'atteins, je lui parle . . ." There follows a moment of
sadness which is at once obliterated by a second wave of recollections:

Prette à entrer dans cette porte, Made de Warens se retourne à ma voix.
Que devins-je à cette vue! Je m'étois figuré une vieille devote bien
rechignée: la bonne Dame de M. de Pontverre ne pouvoit être autre
chose à mon avis. Je vois un visage petri de graces, de beaux yeux bleus
pleins de douceur, un teint eblouissant, le contour d'une gorge enchanteresse. Rien n'échappa au rapide coup d'œil du jeune proselyte; car je
devins à l'instant le sien; sûr qu'une réligion prêchée par de tels missionnaires ne pouvoit manquer de mener en paradis. Elle prend en souriant
la lettre que je lui présente d'une main tremblante, l'ouvre, jette un
coup d'œil sur celle de M. de Pontverre, revient à la mienne, qu'elle lit
tout entiére, et qu'elle eut relue encore, si son laquais ne l'eut avertie
qu'il étoit tems d'entrer. Eh! mon enfant, me dit-elle d'un ton qui me fit
tressaillir, vous voilà courant le pays bien jeune; c'est dommage, en
vérité. Puis sans attendre ma réponse, elle ajoûta: allez chez moi
m'attendre; dites qu'on vous donne à déjeuner: après la messe j'irai
causer avec vous (I, 49).

According to Benedetto's investigation this charming meeting
was in truth no more than "une rencontre banale d'un nouveau
converti et d'une convertisseuse."[6] It is indeed probable that his
interpretation is substantially accurate. Rousseau himself is a hesi-
tant witness, for he seeks to adjust some facts to the needs of his

art which demands the projection of feelings of great expectations and promises as rich as they are undefined. The memory of her tender injunction to *wait for her* is followed by a lengthy account of the life of his patroness cast in terms that suggest an objective evaluation of her vices and virtues. Inserted in this *vita* is a charming portrait of his secular madonna: "Elle avoit un air caressant et tendre, un regard très doux, un sourire angélique, une bouche à la mesure de la mienne, des cheveux cendrés d'une beauté peu commune, et auxquels elle donnoit un tour négligé qui la rendoit très piquante. Elle étoit petite de stature, courte même, et ramassée un peu dans sa taille, quoique sans difformité. Mais il étoit impossible de voir une plus belle tête, un plus beau sein, de plus belles mains et de plus beaux bras" (I, 50). This portrait in the best traditions of eighteenth century French painting—one thinks of Maurice-Quentin de la Tour—gives way to reflections on Mme de Warens' character best summarized by the amazing statement that she had never been the cause of her misfortunes: ". . . elle échouoit par la faute des autres . . ." (I, 51). Having fulfilled his well known promise to omit nothing, Jean-Jacques is presently free to relive this happy hour with the heart of an adolescent and to offer the ingenious testimony of the boy who can scarcely confront the beauty and kindness of the lady before him: "Pauvre petit, tu dois aller où Dieu t'appelle; mais quand tu seras grand tu te souviendras de moi" (I, 53). Such procedures weaken the reader's concern with objective truth. Flattered and disarmed, he is now willing to be charmed by *Maman* as well as to know and miss her in years to come.

Let us accompany Jean-Jacques on his way to Turin:

Je me regardois comme l'ouvrage, l'elève, l'ami, presque l'amant de Mad^e de Warens. Les choses obligeantes qu'elle m'avoit dites, les petites caresses qu'elle m'avoit faites, l'intérest si tendre qu'elle avoit paru prendre à moi, ses regards charmans qui me sembloient pleins d'amour parce qu'ils m'en inspiroient; tout cela nourrissoit mes idées durant la marche, et me faisoit rêver delicieusement. Nulle crainte, nul doute sur mon sort ne troubloit ces rêveries . . . Ainsi je marchois légérement, allégé de ce poids; les jeunes desirs, l'espoir enchanteur, les brillans projets remplissoient mon ame. Tous les objets que je voyois me sembloient les garans de ma prochaine félicité. Dans les maisons j'imaginois des festins rustiques, dans les près de folâtres jeux, le long des eaux, les bains, des promenades, la pêche, sur les arbres des fruits délicieux, sous leurs ombres de voluptueux tête-à-têtes, sur les montagnes des cuves de lait et de crème, une oisiveté charmante, la paix, la simplicité, le plaisir d'aller sans savoir où (I, 58).

Mme de Warens has become a diaphanous element in his *Wunsch-traum*, and to the degree that he yearns for the fulfillment of his indeterminate hopes so characteristic of the pre-romantic and romantic psyches, she will always be associated to those dreams. And whereas the post-romantic yearnings of a Flaubert are invariably accompanied by a sense of loss and impotence as, for example, in *Education Sentimentale*, Rousseau's hopes remain more often unspoiled by mature disenchantment and covert irony. Setting an example for Goethe and Eichendorff, he weaves, as it were, a tapestry of sunlight and happiness.[7] Here he is, about to forego the protection of the Count of Gouvon. The future beckons him and, infatuated with his strange friend Bâcle, he is unable to resist his *Wanderlust*. One cannot but admire his beautiful description of far-off horizons:

Dès lors je ne vis plus d'autre plaisir, d'autre sort, d'autre bonheur que celui de faire un pareil voyage, et je ne voyois à cela que l'inéfable félicité du voyage, au bout duquel, pour surcroit, j'entrevoyois Made de Warens, mais dans un éloignement immense; car pour retourner à Genève, c'est à quoi je ne pensai jamais. Les monts, les prés, les bois, les ruisseaux, les villages se succedoient sans fin et sans cesse avec de nouveaux charmes; ce bienheureux trajet sembloit devoir absorber ma vie entiére (I, 99).

This luminous page offers a fine lesson in how to compose and draw an interior landscape. Indeed, this *paysage intérieur* is a synthesis of the dimensions of space and time, and it may well be that it was Rousseau's intention to arrange the boy's hopes and desires along lines that gradually suggest a perspective leading to Mme de Warens.

"A peine parus-je aux yeux de Made de Warens que son air me rassura. Je tressaillis au prémier son de sa voix, je me précipite à ses pieds, et dans les transports de la plus vive joye je colle ma bouche sur sa main. Pour elle, j'ignore si elle avoit su de mes nouvelles, mais je vis peu de surprise sur son visage, et je n'y vis aucun chagrin. Pauvre petit, me dit-elle d'un ton caressant, te revoila donc? Je savois bien que tu étois trop jeune pour ce voyage; je suis bien aise au moins qu'il n'ait pas aussi mal tourné que j'avois craint" (I, 103, 4). Omniscient, Mme de Warens embodies by now the deep need of protection felt as keenly by those who are young as by those who are old, and to the degree that this hunger for warmth and safety is universal, the average reader cannot but sympathize with the narrator, that is, substitute his feelings of dependency for those of the boy. And it is with incomparable subtlety that Rousseau evokes the tender relationship that may or may not have been lived by himself and his *Maman:* "Dès le premier jour la familiarité la plus douce s'établit entre nous au même dégré où elle a continué tout le reste de sa vie. *Petit* fut mon nom, *Maman* fut le sien, et toujours nous demeurames *Petit* et *Maman*, même quand le nombre des années en eut presque effacé la différence entre nous. Je trouve que ces deux noms rendent à merveilles l'idée de nôtre ton, la simplicité de nos maniéres et surtout la rélation de nos cœurs. Elle fut pour moi la plus tendre des méres qui jamais ne chercha son plaisir mais toujours mon bien; et si les sens entrérent dans mon attachement pour elle, ce n'étoit pas pour en changer la nature, mais pour le rendre seulement plus exquis, pour m'enivrer du charme d'avoir une maman jeune et jolie qu'il m'étoit délicieux de caresser; je dis, caresser au pied de la lettre; car jamais elle n'imagina de m'épargner les baisers ni les plus tendres caresses maternelles, et jamais il n'entra dans mon cœur d'en abuser" (I, 106).

One cannot overstress the thematic innovation that this and like passages represent in the history of European letters. Rousseau's valuation of *la vie intime* has affected the entire nature of the Western symbolic conception and representation of the self in that the individual life becomes the point of departure and end of the psychic quest. Rousseau's *Confessions* are to literature what Van Eyck's portrait is to painting.

Her memory is henceforth the leitmotif of the first part of the *Confessions,* and much of the third book is devoted to an understanding of the Oedipus complex. These analyses are neither short nor decisive—on the contrary, they consist of a series of ideas and impressions which "warm the soul gradually." Nothing is said at once, and all is revealed in a manner that suggests the slow discovery of the secret. Here, for instance, is Jean-Jacques, well established in the house of Mme de Warens: "Cet établissement ne fut pourtant pas encore celui dont je date les jours heureux de ma vie, mais il servit à le préparer" (I, 104). The years go by, and Rousseau furnishes a few details about their tender and chaste relationship still sealed by maternal kisses: "On dira que nous avons pourtant eu à la fin des rélations d'une autre espéce; j'en conviens; mais il faut attendre, je ne puis tout dire à la fois" (I, 106). Thus, the autobiographer insists on surprise, expectation, and eventual discovery, and arranges these feelings in temporal sequences which reinforce the impression of an enigma that betrays its potential of truth.

The following episode confirms the certain effect of such artifice. It is the story of a premonition of happiness which is realized at a later date. Since both premonition and fulfillment take place in the *past*, there is created thereby in the reader's mind a *double past* separated by a false future. The latter is rendered more poignant by false aspirations which release in readers a real nostalgia for a meaningful life:

Je me souviendrai toujours qu'un jour de grande fête, tandis qu'elle étoit à vêpres, j'allai me promener hors de la ville, le cœur plein de son image et du desir ardent de passer mes jours auprès d'elle. J'avois assez de sens pour voir que quand à présent cela n'étoit pas possible, et qu'un bonheur que je goûtois si bien seroit court. Cela donnoit à ma rêverie une tristesse qui n'avoit pourtant rien de sombre et qu'un espoir flateur tempéroit. Le son des cloches qui m'a toujours singulierement affecté, le chant des oiseaux, la beauté du jour, la douceur du paysage, les maisons éparses et champêtres dans lesquelles je plaçois en idée notre commune demeure; tout cela me frappoit tellement d'une impression vive, tendre, triste et touchante, que je me vis comme en extase transporté dans cet heureux tems et dans cet heureux séjour, où mon cœur possédant toute la félicité qui pouvoit lui plaire la goutoit dans des ravissemens inexprimables, sans songer même à la volupté des sens. Je ne me souviens pas de m'être elancé jamais dans l'avenir avec plus de force et d'illusion que je fis alors; et ce qui m'a frappé le plus dans le souvenir de cette rêverie quand elle s'est réalisée, c'est d'avoir retrouvé des objets tels exactement que je les avois imaginés. Si jamais rêve d'un homme éveillé eut l'air d'une vision prophétique, ce fut assurément celui-là. Je n'ai été déçu que dans sa durée imaginaire; car les jours et les ans et la vie entiére s'y passoient dans une inaltérable tranquillité, au lieu qu'en effet tout cela n'a duré qu'un moment. Helas! mon plus constant bonheur fut en songe. Son accomplissement fut presque à l'instant suivi du réveil (I, 107, 8).

This beautiful dream poses a number of psychological questions. Is it not a common occurrence to falsify recollections by means of knowledge obtained at a later date, or to adjust reminiscences to unconscious desires and to marvel after many years about the apparent truth of one's premonitions, which spelled out a future destiny? Thus, one constantly reforms and rearranges recollections in order to account for the life one *has* lived. Yet, such reasoning is not convincing, and I prefer to think that the artist believed in his own divinations, whose very beauty lulls suspicion of invention or pretense. Be that as it may, Rousseau distinguishes between the brief sojourn at the Charmettes and the infinite duration of his dream. This distinction, which is characteristic of Rousseau's philosophy, contrasts real and painful time with imaginary time. The latter, sheltered from disintegration, is the pure duration "où le présent dure toujours sans neanmoins marquer sa durée et sans aucune trace de succession . . ." (Vᵉ Prom., I, 1046). But here is the fulfillment of the prophecy:

La situation d'ame où je me trouvois, tout ce que nous avions dit et fait ce jour-là, tous les objets qui m'avoient frappé me rappellerent l'espéce de rêve que tout éveillé j'avois fait à Annecy sept ou huit ans auparavant et dont j'ai rendu compte en son lieu. Les rapports en étoient si frappans qu'en y pensant j'en fus ému jusqu'aux larmes. Dans un transport d'attendrissement j'embrassai cette chére amie. Maman, maman, lui dis-je avec passion, ce jour m'a été promis depuis longtems, et je ne vois rien au delà (I, 245).

The fourth book begins and ends with two allusions to Mme de Warens, each one in the historical present: "J'arrive et je ne la trouve plus" (I, 132), and "J'arrive enfin, je la revois" (I, 173). They frame one or two years of an adventurous life, whose account is embellished by *l'Idylle des cerises* and enlivened by the anecdote of his concert in Lausanne and that of the *archimandrite* with his "sangue pelasgo." But in respect to *Maman*, who appears to have been angry with her *Petit*, Rousseau is surprisingly silent, except for this confidence:

Il y a longtems que je n'ai parlé de ma pauvre maman; mais si l'on croit que je l'oubliois aussi, l'on se trompe fort. Je ne cessois de penser à elle et de desirer de la retrouver, non seulement pour le besoin de ma subsistance, mais bien plus pour le besoin de mon cœur. Mon attachement pour elle, quelque vif quelque tendre qu'il fut, ne m'empêchoit pas d'en aimer d'autres, mais ce n'étoit pas de la même façon. Toutes devoient également ma tendresse à leurs charmes, mais elle tenoit uniquement à ceux des autres et ne leur eut pas survécu; au lieu que maman pouvoit devenir vieille et laide sans que je l'aimasse moins tendrement . . . Je ne l'aimois ni par devoir ni par intérest ni par convenance; je l'aimois parce que j'étois né pour l'aimer (I, 150, 1).

Despite this loveliest of conclusions, a change of mood is evident. Indeed, this tender indifference tells more of the passage of the years than do dates. *Time is only known and created through its effects;* this, it would seem, is the secret of Rousseau's art.

As if to compensate for his waning erotic passion for *Maman*, Jean-Jacques, in order to maintain her presence in his *readers' mind,* transfers this presence into the landscape henceforth impregnated with her memory, that of his father, and sundry childhood loves:

Toutes les fois que j'approche du pays de Vaud j'éprouve une impression composée du souvenir de Made de Warens qui y est née, de mon pére qui y vivoit, de Melle de Vulson qui y eut les prémices de mon cœur, de plusieurs voyages de plaisir que j'y fis dans mon enfance, et ce me semble, de quelque autre cause encore, plus secrette et plus forte que tout cela. Quand l'ardent désir de cette vie heureuse et douce qui me fuit et pour laquelle j'étois né vient enflammer mon imagination, c'est toujours au pays de Vaud, près du lac, dans des campagnes charmantes qu'elle se fixe (I, 152).

He then enjoins his readers to go to Vevay: ". . . visittez le pays, examinez les sites, promenez-vous sur le lac, et dites si la nature n'a pas fait ce beau pays pour une Julie, pour une Claire, pour un St. Preux; *mais ne les y cherchez pas*" (I, 153, my italics). It is needless to stress that Rousseau's request has not been honored and that Clarens became a place of pilgrimage for many a Romantic author (Goethe, Byron, Shelley *et al.*) failing to heed Rousseau's warning against the pathetic fallacy which he himself had helped to engender.

In the fifth book, the memory of Madame de Warens reaches a peak of intensity: "Je logeai chez moi, c'est à dire chez Maman . . ." (I, 176). In a sense he absorbs her and by the same token, she absorbs him. She alone can save him: "Elle me soigna comme jamais mére n'a soigné son enfant . . ." (I, 221). And elsewhere: "Je devenois tout à fait son œuvre, tout à fait son enfant et plus que si elle eut été ma vraye mére. Nous commençames, sans y songer, à ne plus nous séparer l'un de l'autre, à mettre en quelque sorte *toute notre existence en commun* (my italics), et sentant que reciproquement nous nous étions non seulement necessaires mais suffisans, nous nous accoutumames à ne plus penser à rien d'étranger à nous, à borner absolument notre bonheur et tous nos desirs à cette possession mutuelle et peutetre [sic] unique parmi les humains, qui n'étoit point, comme je l'ai dit, celle de l'amour; mais une possession plus essencielle qui, sans tenir aux sens, au sexe, à l'age, à la figure tenoit à tout ce par quoi l'on est soi, et qu'on ne peut perdre qu'en cessant d'être" (I, 222). Jean-Jacques, child dispossessed by his mother's death, returns once more to the womb of love only to relive again the trauma of his birth, of his *Geworfenheit* into a world far removed from the ideal state of transparency so skillfully analyzed by Jean Starobinski. Implicit in this coming dispossession is the need to share his *Maman* with Claude Anet, his father image, and despite Rousseau's praise of their celebrated *ménage à trois* "Tous nos vœux, nos soins, nos

cœurs étoient en commun" (I, 201), this destruction of his primordial intimacy with his would-be mother, prepares the appearance of Wintzenried who will soon take *his* place. The other
theme foretelling imminent disaster is, to be sure, the resolution
of his Oedipus complex, and it is noteworthy that Rousseau suggests to his readers the sense of his ever-increasing anguish as
gradually as Mme de Warens prepares her pupil for the favors she
intends to bestow upon him. Rousseau's analysis of Mme de
Warens' *méthode* is, moreover, an excellent summary of his
literary technique: "Le jeune homme [the reader, I shall say]
frappé de l'objet qu'on lui présente s'en occupe uniquement, et
saute à pieds joints par dessus vos discours préliminaires pour aller
d'abord où vous le menez trop lentement à son gré. Quand on
veut le rendre attentif il ne faut pas se laisser pénétrer d'avance,
et c'est en quoi Maman fut maladroite" (I, 194). To be sure, our
author is more cunning, for he conceals the real reason for his
anguish. He tergiversates by means of digressions and pretends
to apologize to the reader when the "lecteur, déja révolté" (I, 195)
has already accepted the reality of Rousseau's self-recreation by the
very existence of such objections. Here is the dénouement of this
tragi-comedy: "Comment, par quel prodige dans la fleur de ma
jeunesse eus-je si peu d'empressement pour la prémière jouissance?
Comment pus-je en voir approcher l'heure avec plus de peine que
de plaisir? Comment au lieu des délices qui devoient m'enivrer
sentois-je presque de la répugnance et des craintes?" (I, 195) "A force
de l'appeler maman, à force d'user avec elle de la familiarité d'un
fils je m'étois accoutumé à me regarder comme tel" (I, 196). And
finally this amazing confession: "Je me vis pour la prémiére fois
dans les bras d'une femme, et d'une femme que j'adorois. Fus-je
heureux? Non, je goûtai le plaisir. Je ne sais quelle invincible
tristesse en empoisonnoit le charme. J'étois comme si j'avois commis un inceste" (I, 197).

This avowal, this realization, represents a crucial moment in the
artifical duration of the *Confessions*. Subtle changes indicate that
the objectivized self, that is, the young Jean-Jacques of the book, is
gradually becoming one with Rousseau, author. The autobiographer's attempt to relive his youth transforms itself into a con-
templation of lost years, and the reader senses the gradual ascendancy of the real man, aged, sad, and already illustrious. The beginning of the sixth book exemplifies this change in perspective: "Ici
commence le court bonheur de ma vie; ici viennent les paisibles

mais rapides momens qui m'ont donné le droit de dire que j'ai vécu. Momens précieux et si regrettés, ah recommencez pour moi vôtre aimable cours; coulez plus lentement dans mon souvenir s'il est possible, que vous ne fites reellement dans votre fugitive succession" (I, 225). Henceforth his past is truly past, and the modality of its evocation will be for the most part voluntary save for the celebrated episode of the *pervenche* prophetic of Proust's *madeleine*. Long sequences of verbs in an almost transparent imperfect tense stress the eternity that has been lost: "Je me levois avec le soleil et j'étois heureux; je me promenois et j'étois heureux, je voyois maman et j'étois heureux, je la quittois et j'étois heureux . . ." (I, 225). As if to stress the immensity of his present dispossession, Rousseau conjures up once more the warm presence of Mme de Warens: "Je regardois de loin s'il étoit jour chez maman; quand je voyois son contrevent ouvert, je tressaillois de joye et j'accourois. S'il étoit fermé j'entrois au jardin en attendant qu'elle fut éveillée, m'amusant à repasser ce que j'avois appris la veille ou à jardiner. Le contrevent s'ouvroit; j'allois l'embrasser dans son lit souvent encore à moitié endormie, et cet embrassement aussi pur que tendre tiroit de son innocence même un charme qui n'est jamais joint à la volupté des sens" (I, 236, 7). From now on, however, the outlines of Mme de Warens become indistinct and blurred like that of a former friend seen through the haze of illusory years. Such is the meaning of that short remark "Maman étoit même oubliée" (I, 255) which relates to Rousseau's liaison with Mme de Larnage. It presages his irrevocable break with Mme de Warens who, on having taken her new lover Wintzenried, receives her former *protégé* coldly and politely. Indeed, Rousseau's lament, *gidien avant la lettre:* "Comment vivre étranger dans la maison dont j'étois l'enfant" (I, 270) shows to what degree *Maman*'s home had been Rousseau's church. And when we read that Jean-Jacques, after his return from Lyon where he had been the tutor of M. de Mably's children, had come to find "the past which was no more and which could not rise again" (I, 270, my trans.), we know that these are the feelings of a man who has lost his youth. I should add that such is also the viewpoint of the artist, who realizes the need to change the mode of his self-recreation by rediscovering henceforth the real past instead of being reborn into an artificial future.

The second part of the *Confessions* hardly alludes to Mme de Warens. Her memory reappears painfully as Thérèse Levasseur enters Rousseau's life: "Il falloit, pour tout dire, un successeur à Maman; puisque je ne devois plus vivre avec elle il me falloit quelqu'un qui vécut avec son élève, et en qui je trouvasse la simplicité, la docilité de cœur qu'elle avoit trouvée en moi . . . Quand j'étois absolument seul mon cœur étoit vide, mais il n'en falloit qu'un pour le remplir. Le sort m'avoit ôté, m'avoit aliéné du moins en partie, celui pour lequel la nature m'avoit fait" (I, 331, 2). And when he mentions Mme de Warens again, Rousseau insists on the decay of her faculties and on the fall of her virtues: "Déja le sentiment de sa misére lui resseroit le cœur et lui retrecissoit l'esprit" (I, 339). He meets her again in 1754, when she is fifty-four years of age: ". . . dans quel état, mon Dieu! quel avilissement! que lui restoit-il de sa vertu prémiére? Etoit-ce la même Made de Warens jadis si brillante à qui le Curé Pontverre m'avoit adressé? Que mon cœur fut navré!" (I, 391). Confronted by the choice of returning to her, he concludes: "Je gémis sur elle et ne la suivis pas" (I, 392). Comfortably installed at the *Hermitage,* he meditates in a similar vein: "La soif du bonheur ne s'éteint point dans le cœur de l'homme. Maman vieillissoit et s'avilissoit. Il m'étoit prouvé qu'elle ne pouvoit plus être heureuse ici-bas. Restoit à chercher un bonheur qui me fut propre, ayant perdu tout espoir de jamais partager le sien" (I, 413). During the same period, he encounters Venture, who had been the mundane idol of his boyhood, and he bemoans once more, as will Proust, the passing of the years:

J'eus à peu près dans le même tems une visite à laquelle je ne m'attendois guéres, quoique ce fut une bien ancienne connoissance. Je parle de mon ami Venture, qui vint me surprendre un beau matin, lorsque je ne pensois à rien moins. Un autre homme étoit avec lui. Qu'il me parut changé! Au lieu de ses anciennes graces je ne lui trouvai plus qu'un air crapuleux, qui m'empêcha de m'épanouir avec lui . . . Je le vis presque avec indifférence, et nous nous séparames assez froidement. Mais quand il fut parti le souvenir de nos anciennes liaisons me rappella si vivement celui de mes jeunes ans, si doucement, si sagement consacrés à cette femme angélique qui maintenant n'étoit guéres moins changée que lui . . . (I, 398).

Henceforth the *Confessions* disregard the destiny of Mme de Warens. From time to time, there surge forth memories of *Les Charmettes,* which have found expression in *La Nouvelle Héloïse.* But the tenth and eleventh books do not even mention the name of his former benefactress, whom Rousseau abandoned to a pitiful fate: "Je méritai par là les châtimens terribles qui depuis lors n'ont cessé de m'accabler . . ." (I, 392). Despite this remorse, the very end of the eulogy composed for Mme de Warens shows that she had become in many ways but a supplement to the powerful ego of the author, who often envisaged his fellow men as being lifeless masses moved by obscure forces. The style of the panegyric is mellifluous and reminiscent of Fénelon. However, these unctuous exaggerations soon give way to complacent self-commiserations.

Ma seconde perte, plus sensible encore et bien plus irréparable fut celle de la meilleure des femmes et des méres qui déja chargée d'ans et surchargée d'infirmités et de miséres quitta cette Vallée de larmes pour passer dans le séjour des bons, où l'aimable souvenir du bien qu'on a fait ici bas en fait l'éternelle récompense. Allez, ame douce et bienfaisante auprès des Fénelon, des Bernex, des Catinat, et de ceux qui dans un état plus humble ont ouvert comme eux leurs cœurs à la charité véritable, allez goûter le fruit de la vôtre et préparer à votre élève la place qu'il espère un jour occuper près de vous. Heureuse, dans vos infortunes que le Ciel en les terminant vous ait épargné le cruel spectacle des siennes (I, 619, 620).

Mme de Warens died in 1762.[8] That same year, Rousseau began his exile in Switzerland and England, leading a life of anxiety which finally became one of gentle appeasement. In 1778, Rousseau begins the last page of *la dixième promenade* of his *Rêveries:* "Aujourdui jour de paques fleuries il y a precisement cinquante ans de ma prémiére connoissance avec Made de Warens" (I, 1098). Destiny and poetry at last unite: "Ah! si j'avois suffi à son cœur comme elle suffisoit au mien! Quels paisibles et délicieux jours nous eussions coulés ensemble! Nous en avons passé de tels mais qu'ils ont été courts et rapides, et quel destin les a suivis! Il n'y a pas de jour où je ne me rappelle avec joye et attendrissement cet unique et court tems de ma vie où je fus moi pleinement sans mélange et sans obstacle et où je puis véritablement dire avoir vécu" (I, 1098, 9). Past are the uncertainties of existence and gone the illusions of his art. Resolved is the contradiction between semblance and reality. There is left for Rousseau only the memory of love and the vain intention to have wanted one day "to pay back to the best of women the good deeds she had done him" (I, 1099).[9]

CHAPTER II

Rousseau's *Idylle des Cerises*—A Metamorphosis of the Pastoral Ideal

> "Que j'aime à tomber de tems en tems sur les momens agréables de ma jeunesse? Ils m'étoient si doux; ils ont été si courts, si rares, et je les ai goûtés à si bon marché! Ah leur seul souvenir rend encore à mon cœur une volupté pure dont j'ai besoin pour ranimer mon courage, et soutenir les ennuis du reste de mes ans." (*Confessions*)
>
> "La poésie lui rappelait le temps pastoral." (*Fragments sur J. J. Rousseau*, Bernardin de Saint-Pierre)
>
> ". . . ja jeder einzelne Mensch hat sein Paradies, sein goldnes Zeitalter. (Schiller)

"Chante moy d'une musette bien resonnante et d'une fluste bien jointe ces plaisantes ecclogues rustiques, à l'exemple de Thëocrit et de Virgile, marines, à l'exemple de Sennazar, gentilhomme nëapolitain . . ."[1] That du Bellay's poetical imperative went unheeded is history. No French pastoral in the Italian tradition, be it Marot's *Complaincte de Madame de Loyse de Savoye* or Racan's *Bergeries* can rival Garcilaso's first *Egloga* or Tasso's *Aminta,* while d'Urfée's *Astrée* has received honorable mention in default of worthy competition in Italy, Spain, and England. And should this affirmation seem unjustified, one may quote by way of *Deffence* Mia Gerhardt's conclusion to her general survey of the pastoral genre: "En France . . . la pastorale ne réussit pas à s'implanter dans le roman, et reste fort médiocre dans la poésie; la pastorale dramatique apparaît comme la forme la plus en accord avec les tendances de la littérature française et la plus goûtée du public, mais elle n'a pas abouti à une œuvre de premier ordre."[2] Are we to conclude that there is no "usignuolo / Che va di ramo in

17

ramo / Cantando: Io amo, io amo"[3] in the gardens of French
literature, and that we have to content ourselves with Mallarmé's
version of the *Sicilian Muse?* Should we agree with Bernardin de
Saint-Pierre that "malheureusement, nous n'avons pas eu de poètes
épiques ni bucoliques . . . ?"[4] If one allows an exception to this
rule, it would surely have to be Bernardin de Saint-Pierre's friend,
Jean-Jacques Rousseau, who, as a matter of principle, fancied himself different from all men. However this may be, it is the sense
of this essay that Rousseau was the first European writer to have
succeeded in modernizing the pastoral idyll[5] which had been for
the most patterned on the Graeco-Italian and to a lesser extent
on the Christian pastoral ideal.[6]

Jean-Jacques leaves little doubt that, as a boy, he was passion-
ately involved with *Le Grand Cyrus* and *l'Astrée,* only to abandon
them for Plutarch's *Lives:* "Le plaisir que je prenois à le [Plu-
tarque] relire sans cesse me guerit un peu des Romans, et je
préferai bientôt Agesilas, Brutus, Aristide à Orodante, Artamene
et Juba" (I, 9).[7] Although the influence of pastoral novels on
Rousseau has been studied, his role as an innovator in the pastoral
genre has been disregarded by scholars, with the notable exception
of the late Renato Poggioli whose views approach mine.[8] Rereading
the libretto of Rousseau's *Devin du Village* this neglect seems
quite understandable: "Mon chalumeau, ma houlette, / Soyez mes
seules grandeurs" (II, 1105). This doggerel summarizes his early
aspirations; and with such lines in mind, Jules Marsan may have
been justified in ending his *Pastorale dramatique française* with a
commentary on le *Berger Extravagant,* 1627: "Nous pouvons
arrêter ici cette histoire de la pastorale dramatique: son rôle est
terminé, et, si son influence persiste, la plupart de ceux-mêmes qui
la subissent—très indirectement—sont les premiers à les mépriser."[9]

Just as Rousseau's mediocrity as an author of traditional pastorals lends no support to the thesis that he is the creator of the
modern idyll, so his avowed lack of classical training "je ne sais
point le grec et très peu le latin"[10] seems to invalidate my basic
argument. And while it is true that a good deal has been written
on the impact of Plato, Socrates, Lucretius, Plutarch, Tacitus, and
Seneca on the ideology of the Citizen of Geneva, still, if one compares him to Voltaire and Diderot, who were excellent classical
scholars in their own right, one would have to conclude that in
his case it is unwarranted to speak of well-defined Greek literary
influences. The question of indirect classical literary influences is

more difficult to resolve. Although there exists a fairly complete inventory of Rousseau's library, it is evident that we cannot limit the number of Greek authors he read in translation to those in his possession; the list compiled by M. Reichenburg, for example, does not mention either Theocritus or Longus.[11] In view of the fact that Rousseau's early works teem with pastoral stock characters we may assume that he had read Amyot's translation of the celebrated Alexandrian tale. But in regard to indirect classical literary influences transmuted and transmitted by Italian literature, one is less dependent on conjecture, since studies by Culcasi, Benedetto, and Beal suggest the extent of Rousseau's indebtedness to the *cinquecento* and *settecento*.[12] He knew and loved Italian; his preference was for Ariosto, Tasso and Metastasio; his favorite work was *La Gerusalemme liberata;* and he was acquainted moreover with *l'Aminta*—the point of confluence of the classical pastoral tradition and the apogee of the Renaissance pastoral ideal— which may have exerted a subtle influence upon the composition of *l'Idylle des Cerises.*

Rousseau's originality in reformulating the traditional pastoral can best be shown by means of a preliminary analysis of the thematic components of *l'Idylle*.[13] Its beginning refers specifically to Midsummer Eve, "the turning point of the year," as Frazer remarks, "when vegetation might be thought to share the incipient though still almost imperceptible decay of summer, and which might very well be chosen by primitive man as a fit moment for resorting to those magic rites by which he hopes to stay the decline, or at least to ensure the revival, of plant life."[14] Thus Rousseau:

L'aurore un matin me parut si belle que m'étant habillé précipitamment, je me hâtai de gagner la campagne pour voir lever le soleil. Je goutai ce plaisir dans tout son charme; c'étoit la semaine après la St. Jean. La terre dans sa plus grande parure étoit couverte d'herbe et de fleurs; les rossignols presque à la fin de leur ramage sembloient se plaire à le renforcer: tous les oiseaux faisant en concert leurs adieux au printems, chantoient la naissance d'un beau jour d'été, d'un de ces beaux jours qu'on ne voit plus à mon age, et qu'on n'a jamais vu dans le triste sol où j'habite aujourd'hui (I, 135).

In melodious prose the *Idylle* evokes the universal grief of nature and the lament of the nightingales on the passing of Spring with a graceful stylistic *chute* suggestive of exile and death. One might note in passing that this feeling of sadness at the destruction of tender life may have engendered the myth of Daphnis, inventor of the bucolic song: "Auch wir suchen die ersten Keime der Daphnis-sage in uralter Naturanschauung, wir sehen in ihm einen jener zahlreichen schönen, früh verblassten Knaben oder Jünglinge, welche das fröhliche Aufblühen des Naturlebens im Lenze und das von den Menschen betrauerte und beklagte Verwelken der Vegetation in den heissen Tagen der Sommerzeit darstellen (Hylas, Linos, Narkissos u.a.)."[15] Later developments of the myth relate how Daphnis, cherished by muses and nymphs, boasted of being able to withstand the power of Eros, that Aphrodite caused him to love a young girl and that, struggling without hope against this passion, he died despite a vain attempt by the goddess to save him.

Superimposed on these schemas and rituals in *l'Idylle* is the myth of the Golden Age which had first been integrated into the pastoral tradition in Virgil's fourth *Eclogue*. Whereas the latter's Golden Age is about to return—*redeunt Saturnia regna*—and Tasso's is voluptuously present "E veramente il secol d'oro è questo . . . ,"[16] Rousseau's *Idylle* shimmers with the light of a Golden Age long since past: "Und Strahlen aus der schönern Zeit / Haben die Boten dein Herz gefunden."[17] Whether Virgil believed in his Arcadia must remain a matter of conjecture; it is certain, however, that Jean-Jacques wanted to believe in his Alpine Arcadia, and that the discrepancy between his reminiscence of rustic innocence and the miseries of exile in England creates contrapuntal moods. Like Tasso, whom he thought the equal of Homer and Virgil, Rousseau animates his pastoral idyll with powerful feelings. Unlike Tasso, he does not people his world with shepherds, nymphs, goddesses and the like, but fills it with projections of himself and his youthful loves, maintaining all the while the essential patterns that sustain the pastoral. It might be argued that in dispensing with shepherds Rousseau destroys the essence of the pastoral, since its high degree of conscious artificiality represents the very essence of the genre. In the words of Mia Gerhardt: "L'écrivain pastoral est, par définition, un *artifex*, celui qui *fait de l'art;* la pastorale est artificielle, non seulement dans l'acceptation courante du mot, qui ne présente aucun intérêt, mais dans son sens propre et étymologique."[18] If the pastoral had always been what it became after Virgil transformed it into a vehicle for allegory, our interpretation of *l'Idylle des Cerises* would not be defensible. But the Theocritan tradition preëmpts the Virgilian, and we hope to show that Rousseau drew on both traditions by way of Italy in order to fashion the modern idyll.

The first sentence after the prologue illustrates the technique of modernization through the elimination of some, although not all, Virgilian and Italian Renaissance literary devices. This allows him to render his version of the pastoral more *vraisemblable*—a vital necessity for Rousseau, since the credibility of the *Moi* he wishes to project must not suffer through overt mythopoeic artifacts: "Je m'étois insensiblement éloigné de la Ville . . ." As in Longus' *Daphnis and Chloë*, contrasts between city and country life function as a device to permit urbane readers to peek into a utopian garden where hero and heroine play at love without understanding the game. That Rousseau added a second heroine renders the situation the more piquant, and it takes little insight to recognize in this *idylle à trois* a reversal of the Madame de Warens-Claude Anet-Jean-Jacques triangle.[19] Less apparent, perhaps, is the fact that this supposedly fortuitous meeting of a commoner with two aristocratic girls, reflects an unusual reversal of a pattern characteristic of the *pastourelle* which usually relates with more or less irony how a knight encounters a "gentil pastorele, / les eux verz, le chief blondel," with varying degrees of success. If one assumes that the French pastoral tradition of the seventeenth century resulted from a fusion of a national tradition *en langue d'oïl* (typified by the prevalence of a strong caste system and disdain towards peasants with the consecrated exception of the *Jeu de Robin et Marion*) with the Graeco-Italian tradition in turn characterized by democratic attitudes,[20] *l'Idylle des Cerises* offers a fascinating example of a thematic metamorphosis. In *l'Idylle* Rousseau avails himself of a native pattern (the knight versus the *pastoure*), assumes the role of the *pastoure* and halves the figure of *li chevaliers* into two *cavalières*. He also appropriates egalitarian beliefs from Tasso's *Aminta* and obviates at the same time any possible accusation of being a *paysan parvenu* by being delightfully shy after having led the horses across the stream.

"Vous vous étes mouillé pour notre service; nous devons en conscience avoir soin de vous sécher: il faut s'il vous plait venir avec nous, nous vous arrêtons prisonnier . . . montez en croupe derriére elle, nous voulons rendre compte de vous. Mais Mademoiselle, je n'ai point l'honneur d'être connu de Madame votre mere . . ." (I, 136). Thus, the two amazones seduce on a level as virtual as virtuous Jean-Jacques who does not content himself with being a latter-day *pastoure,* but assumes the role of the satyr as well as the function of the autobiographer. But whereas Tasso's *satiro* is an eloquent spokesman for the libido ". . . e queste mie velate coscie / son di virilità, di robustezza indicio,"[21] young Jean-Jacques rather creates the impression of a *petit satyre* in need of wine to hold his own with *Mlles les bacchantes*. Obviously, the interlude is not devoid of erotic implications; but, as usual, Rousseau mutes sensuous effects, and readers uninterested in courtship *more Platonico* will have to wait for the idyll of Monsieur Dudding and Mme de Larnage before meeting a *satiro* and *Dafne* worthy of Tasso.

Closer to the subject-matter is the problem of the structure of *l'Idylle des Cerises* and its relation to the structure of the pastoral. That the eclogue is inherently dramatic has become a critical commonplace. In the words of W. W. Greg: ". . . of the Idyls of Theocritus only about a third contains more than one character; of Vergil's *Bucolics* at least half; of Calpurnius' all but one; of the eclogues of Petrarch and Boccaccio all without exception."[22] How the dramatic pastoral developed from the recited eclogue still remains a matter of controversy. It is certain, however, that the pastoral dramas and novels of the sixteenth and seventeenth centuries came to be characterized by a rigid organization of human relationships. This equilibrium, this changelessness, results from the fact that interaction among *la chaîne des amants* as, for instance, in *Il Pastor Fido* or *La Diana,* is governed by abstract principles determined by myths and traditions. That Tasso, Jonson, and Shakespeare were able to dramatize these principles, to breathe new life into stereotypes, can only be ascribed to their genius—Scene 1 of Act III and Scene 1 of Act IV between Ferdinand and Miranda in *The Tempest* being examples of a dazzling metamorphosis of worn pastoral myths and legends. This supremacy of essentially static principles over psychodynamic principles of the sort which animate, for example, *La Princesse de Clèves* accounts for the eventual failure of the pastoral drama and novel. *L'Idylle des Cerises* exhibits the characteristically static quality of the pastoral without being lifeless, since the lack of overt action by the *dramatis personae* is compensated by a powerful flow of energy emanating from the narrator. Having suppressed all excessive developments in terms of intrigue, allegory, and pastoral conventions, and having reduced the number of characters to three, Rousseau organized his confessional data according to the canons of French classical drama. The *Idylle* consists of five parts framed by a prologue and epilogue and observes strictly the rules of the unities.[23] By virtue of this remarkable simplification and by making himself the source of feeling Rousseau succeeded two thousand years after Theocritus in creating a modern idyll woven of sunlight and shade, resounding with laughter and echoing with an ancient strain of happiness and love.

It is noteworthy that the *mise en scène* of *l'Idylle des Cerises* conforms to Curtius' definition of Virgil's *Ideallandschaft* rather than to Theocritus' landscape. The latter's setting, studded with precise details, trembles in the heat of summer: "On the shady boughs the dusky cicadas were busy with their chatter, and the tree-frog far off cried in the dense thornbrake. Larks and finches sang, the dove made moan, and bees flitted humming about the springs. All things were fragrant of rich harvest and of fruit-time."[24] Virgil, while drawing on Theocritus "makes no attempt to match his model in visual richness, in the full scale of sounds and odors. Augustan classicism does not tolerate Hellenistic color-fulness."[25] The parallel between Rousseau and Virgil is obvious—both lived in an age that looked askance on realistic elaboration in favor of stylized outlines. Flowers, trees, summer heat, shade and a brook—these constitute the *locus amoenus* and Rousseau's little picture (*eidyllion*)[26] exhibits a surprising degree of correspondance with this nature topos. But whereas in most of his eclogues Virgil escapes to a faraway Arcadia he had never seen, Rousseau returns, like Theocritus, to the landscape of his boyhood. One should add that *l'Idylle des Cerises* unfolds exclusively in daylight in contrast to *l'Aminta, Favola Boschereccia*, which, according to Tortoretto "è tutta idillio (purissimo idillio) . . ."[27] In it, attention is focused on the sylvan setting where sunlight filters through leaves and branches allowing Tasso to suggest visions that defy illumination: "Silvia t'attende a un fonte, ignuda e sola."[28] However tempted Rousseau might have been by such *voluttà idillica*, he conceived his idyll in praise of purity: *la volupté morale réclame la lumière* or, in Miltonian terms:

> What hath night to do with sleep?
> Night hath better sweets to prove,
> Venus now wakes, and wak'ns Love.
> Come let us our rites begin,
> 'Tis only daylight that makes Sin.[29]

"Nous nous aimions sans mistére et sans honte et nous voulions nous aimer toujours ainsi" (I, 138). This triad of *amour-mystère-honte* invites pleasing meditations on *la pudeur à la chrétienne* that stresses polarities between spiritual and sensuous love—a contrast which dovetails with other pastoral oscillations between town and country, the Age of Gold and that of Iron, reality and unreality. In Tasso's *Aminta,* dynamic tension results from the dramatic juxtaposition of the chaste Aminta and Silvia· (Vossler calls her "ein sprödes Nymphchen")[30] with the experienced and disenchanted twosome of Tirsis and Dafne flanked by the satyr. Parenthetically, one should add that Milton's *Comus,* obviously influenced by Shakespeare's *Midsummer Night's Dream* and George Peele's *Old Wives' Tale,* bears, according to Mario Praz, the imprint of Tasso's *Aminta* whose tension, essentially poetic, has been intensified by moral fervor: "Tasso's pastoral, with its tender atmosphere, its passion, and its despairs gushing out so easily . . . has been transformed almost beyond recognition into a morality in antique garb."[31] Garcilaso's first *Egloga* "O más dura que mármol a mis quejas . . . ," Cervantes' *Galatea,* and Lope's *Arcadia* exhibit similar polarities fashioned of dialectical conceits and allusions:

> O ausencia, madre inútil de memorias . . .

But, whereas the Italian, the Englishman, and the Spaniards achieve poetic tension, respectively, through reliance on pre-existing mythopeic and Christian value-systems, Rousseau dispenses with overt references to tradition in favor of a referential system based solely on *his* Ego. I suggested that in his *Idylle des Cerises* he is a man of many parts; it should be manifest that he is also a man of many values, specifically, of purity and impurity, and that his role of value-giver, although non-Christian, poses thorny problems. It is relatively simple for a Dante or a Claudel to conjure up the immaculate silhouettes of Beatrice or *La Jeune Fille Violaine,* since these figures represent religious and poetic beliefs and fantasies for authors and readers. One's Ego, however, is not a fantasy, and to declare that it is pure is to contradict the realities of life in which Egos are inextricably involved and determined by value systems (cultures) and value-makers (parents) over which they have no control. "Or, la pureté est une qualité morale qui ne tolère pas le Je," states Vladimir Jankélévitch: "Comme Dieu, dont nul ne peut nommer le nom ni supporter la vue, la pureté exige en quelque sorte un regard oblique."[32] How does Rousseau resolve psychologically the twofold problem of 1. projecting the presence of a pure, absolutely independent Ego "transparent comme le cristal," 2. establishing an oblique point of view *on* himself *by* himself, permitting the process of individuation, the *sine qua non* of autobiography? Most students of Rousseau's life, friendly, or hostile, will immediately suggest Rousseau's solution: self-deification.[33] If his absolute purity and goodness necessitate his being God, he will be God, and, in order to achieve an oblique viewpoint concerning "himself" (i.e., the inner distance between the *Moi* that writes in an incessantly evanescent present and the *Moi* that lived happily and purely in a past far removed), Rousseau postulates that he *was* the Son of God who lived and died in times that bear no relation to a sorrowful present.[34]

It is, of course, possible to relate directly Jean-Jacques' "amour sans mistére et sans honte" to Calvinist and Catholic dogmas as well as to sixteenth-century neo-platonism as formulated by Leo Hebreo's *Dialoghi d'Amore* and Castiglione's *Cortegiano*—doctrines that reached Rousseau through *l'Astrée* by way of *La Diana*. Montemayor's doctrinal pronouncements on *la liempeza del amor* offer some of the ingredients of Rousseau's formula, but none of its charms, since the trinity of *amour-mystère-honte* also revives delightful memories of forbidden fruit on the tree of knowledge which Jean-Jacques wastes no time in climbing:

> Je montai sur l'arbre et je leur en jettois des bouquets dont elles me rendoient les noyaux à travers les branches. Une fois Mlle Galley avançant son tablier et reculant la tête se présentoit si bien, et je visai si juste, que je lui fis tomber un bouquet dans le sein; et de rire. Je me disois en moi-même; que mes levres ne sont-elles des cérises! comme je les leur jetterois ainsi de bon cœur? (I, 137)

Flawless lines with anacreontic overtones lead to the climax of *l'Idylle des Cerises* whose end—*Auflösung* would be a more fitting term—is more in the tradition of Virgil's *Eclogues* than of Theocritus' *Idylls* which owing to their unsentimentality avoid grief or melancholy. The ransom of feeling is sadness: "Iam summa procul villarum culmina fumant / maioresque cadunt altis de montibus umbrae."[35] The light of day fades: "Enfin elles se souvinrent qu'il ne falloit pas attendre la nuit pour rentrer en ville . . . En marchant nous disions que la journée avoit tort de finir . . ." (I, 138). Through a series of gradations the inner distance between Jean-Jacques the boy and Rousseau the writer increases to the point where the adventure becomes a luminescent moment outside of time, a source of consolation to himself and others: "Pour moi je sais que la mémoire d'un si beau jour me touche plus, me charme plus, me revient plus au cœur que celle d'aucuns plaisirs que j'aye goutés en ma vie" (I, 138). And *l'Idylle* ends on a note of finality that severs the dream from reality lest it be destroyed by it: "Quoiqu'il en soit, il me sembloit en les quittant que je ne pourrois plus vivre sans l'une et sans l'autre. Qui m'eut dit que je ne les reverrois de ma vie, et que là finiroient nos éphémeres amours?" (I, 139)

Up to now we have interpreted *l'Idylle* in the light of classical, medieval, and Renaissance antecedents, particularly theme, structure, and intent. Before considering romantic and post-romantic idylls derived from, and influenced by, *l'Idylle des Cerises*, we should refer to neo-classical theories on the pastoral genre by Rapin, Fontenelle and Samuel Johnson. Rapin admits his perplexity with disarming candor: "But tis hard to give *Rules* for that, for which there have been none already given; for where there are no footsteps nor path to direct, I cannot tell how any one can be certain of his way. Yet in this difficulty I will follow *Aristotle*'s Example, who being unable to lay down Rules concerning *Epicks*, propos'd Homer as a Pattern, from whom he deduc'd the whole Art: So I will gather from *Theocritus* and *Virgil*, these Fathers of *Pastoral*, what I shall deliver on this account." But unlike the Stagirite, the Jesuit priest contents himself with formulating axioms that appear quite self-evident: "But as a glorious *Heroick* action must be the Subject of an *Heroick* Poem, so a *Pastoral* action of a Pastoral . . ."[36] Fontenelle, rationalist on all counts, directs his *Discours sur la nature de l'églogue,* 1688, generally against *les Anciens* and specifically against Rapin "contre ceux qui professent cette espèce de religion que l'on s'est faite d'adorer l'antiquité . . ."[37] His criteria are to be "les lumières naturelles de la Raison" and they reveal, like his *Histoire des Oracles,* his enlightened misunderstanding of the poetic power of myth and imagination. His objection that Theocritus' shepherds "sentent trop la campagne"[38] and that their behavior is reprehensible will be echoed by Dr. Johnson's insistence on "Chastity of sentiment . . . and Purity of Manners."[39] In fairness to neo-classical critics, it must be stated that the relative lack of doctrine concerning the pastoral genre invites idiosyncratic views and that, according to Greg, confusion among critics is intensified by the fact that "any definition sufficiently elastic to include the protean forms assumed by what we call the 'pastoral ideal' could hardly have sufficient intention to be of any real value."[40] However, one has to take issue with Greg when he identifies *definition* with *theory* and concludes his valuable treatise on *Pastoral Poetry and Drama* with an *a priori* rejection of the possibility of a theory of the pastoral: "It cannot be too emphatically laid down that there is and can be no such thing as a 'theory' of pastoral, or, indeed, of any other artistic form dependent, like it, upon what are merely accidental conditions." Had he turned to Herder,[41] Schiller, and Jean Paul his conclusion might have been less adamant.

Indeed, the essay *Über naive und sentimentalische Dichtung,* 1795, offers a celebrated instance of a theory on the idyll as well as *Hirtenidylle,* and it is somewhat surprising that the indexes of Cararra, Greg, Marson, Hulubei, and Gerhardt should mention neither Schiller nor Jean Paul, although both attempted, aside from analyzing the idyll, to lay a theoretical foundation which makes possible a reformulation of the pastoral to adjust it to contemporary life.[42]

Space does not permit me to outline all aspects of this important critical problem, and discussion of Schiller's views must be limited to a few passages relevant to Rousseau. After distinguishing the naive poet from the sentimental poet (the former *is* nature, the latter seeks it), he proceeds to characterize satirical, elegiac, and idyllic poetry. Discussing the genre of the modern elegy, he writes: "Rousseau, whether considered as a poet or a philosopher, always obeys the same tendency; to seek nature or to avenge it by art. According to the state of his heart, whether he prefers to seek nature or to avenge it, we see him at one time roused by elegiac feelings, at others showing the tone of the satire of Juvenal; and again, as in his Julia [*La Nouvelle Héloïse*], delighting in the sphere of the idyll."[43] Granting that his compositions have poetic value, Schiller accuses Jean-Jacques of always betraying "a want of physical *repose* rather than a want of moral harmony" and of preferring "to place the aim nearer the earth, and to lower the ideal in order to reach it the sooner and the safer."[44] After analyzing Kleist, Haller, and Klopstock in his terms, Schiller enounces a theory of the idyll which fits, *sur mesure,* as it were, my argument which views Rousseau as the modernizer of the classical idyll. "The end of the idyll," argues Schiller, "is to portray man in a state of innocence which means a state of harmony and peace with himself and the external world. But a state such as this is not merely met with before the dawn of civilization; it is also the state to which civilization aspires, as to its last end, if only it obeys a determined tendency in its progress. The idea of a similar state, and the belief of the possible reality of this state, is the only thing that can reconcile man with all the evils to which he is exposed in the path of civilization . . ."[45] And with such Rousseauean theses in mind, the poet-philosopher views the idyll as a proof of the possibility of human harmony and peace: "It is, therefore, of infinite importance for the man engaged in the path of civilization to see confirmed in a sensuous manner the belief that this idea can be accomplished in the world of sense, that this state of innocence can be realized in it . . ."[46] Unfortunately, argues Schiller, the classical idyll "places *behind us* the end towards which *it ought to lead us,* and consequently it can only inspire us with the sad feeling of a loss, and not the joyous feeling of a hope [author's italics]." It behooves, therefore, the modern poet to create a harmonious emancipation: "Let him prepare as his task an idyll that realizes pastoral innocence, even in the children of civilization, and in all the conditions of the most militant and excited life; of thought enlarged by culture; of the most refined art; of the most delicate social conventionalities—an idyll, in short, that is made, not to bring back man to *Arcadia,* but to lead him to *Elysium.*"[47] In his instructive essay Horst Rüdiger underlines the eschatalogical nature of Schiller's visions: "Wo aber liegt jene *andere Welt,* welche der sentimentalischen Dichtung allein angemessen ist? Sie liegt—daran kann nach der bisherigen Analyse des Schillerschen Gedankens kein Zweifel sein—in der Zukunft, genauer: in einer eschatalogischen Zukunft, in jenem idealen Reiche also, dem Schiller die treffende sinnbildliche Bezeichnung Elysium gibt: 'Gefilde der Hinkunft' bedeutet der Name. Diesem Reiche steht *Arkadien* als 'poetisches Ideogramm' für die Urvergangenheit des Hirtentumus gegenüber."[48]

That Schiller considered Voss' *Luise* as an approximation of his ideals seems a forgivable error in judgment; what matters is his emphasis on modernization, although his neo-Kantian and to some extent pre-Fichtean orientation led him to relate the idyll to an ideal with chiliastic implications.[49]

Less theoretical are Jean Paul's aesthetic considerations on the idyll which he defines as the "epische Darstellung des Vollglücks in der Beschränkung"[50]—a felicitious definition that frees the idyll from traditional pastoral conventions and Schiller's eschatalogical conditions and relates it to Rousseau: "Sogar das Leben des Robinson Crusoe und das des Jean-Jacques auf seiner Peters-Insel erquickt uns mit Idyllen-Duft und Schmelz." Any serene moment, the holiday of a teacher, the baptism of a first child: ". . . alle diese Tage können Idylle werden und können singen: auch wir waren in Arkadien."[51] The only conditions that limit his definition are that idylls must not be "clouded by passion, nor written by Gessner or a Frenchman . . ."[52]

With these ideas in mind, it is not surprising that Jean Paul should have turned to Jean-Jacques for confirmation of his theory on the possibility of idylls suitable for modern man. Elsewhere, I have stated that it is Rousseau's greatness to have sought a re-evaluation of values in regard to the self, the family, and the state, not by having recourse to transcendental agents, but by exploiting neglected values. That these values include *le bonheur* will be disputed by few though many have cast doubt on its reality. Indeed, Rousseau, who often thought himself the most wretched of men, assumes the tragic role of the champion of human happiness and the intention which created *l'Idylle des Cerises* answers this vocation. But whereas his case for "happiness" in *l'Idylle des Charmettes* [weakened by his need to tell things "comme il [lui] sembloit qu'elles avoient du être" (I, 1035)] and to a lesser degree in his *Lettres à Malesherbes* and the *Rêveries,* forms part of a deep and powerful current of feeling, *l'Idylle des Cerises* seems to be shored up, as it were, against the ebb and flow of despair and ecstasy. It is "das Vollglück in der Beschränkung" which results from a completely original fusion of the pastoral schema derived from Theocritus, Virgil, and Tasso with his personal dream of salvation and peace—a *Vollglück* that is a harmonious reconciliation of classical order and pre-romantic plenitude.

It is important to distinguish clearly the structural differences between *l'Idylle des Cerises* and *l'Idylle des Charmettes* which posits happiness exclusively within the heart and mind of one person, proclaiming in a pastoral setting, a state of emotional self-sufficiency: "Je me levois avec le soleil et j'étois heureux; je me promenois et j'étois heureux, je voyois Maman et j'étois heureux, je la quittois et j'étois heureux, je parcourois les bois, les coteaux, j'errois dans les vallons, je lisois, j'étois oisif, je travaillois au jardin, je cueillois les fruits, j'aidois au ménage, et le bonheur me suivoit par tout; il n'étoit dans aucune chose assignable, il étoit tout en moi-même, il ne pouvoit me quitter un seul instant" (I, 225, 6). Devoid of all dramatic tension, these celebrated lines state as a matter of simple fact that he, Rousseau, had known happiness.

Forgetting St. Augustine and Pascal, and remembering perhaps Montaigne[53] and through him Epicurus in his garden, Jean-Jacques evokes and idyllizes a state of being that approaches the *autarkeia* of the Cynics and Stoics. Similarily, *La cinquième rêverie du promeneur solitaire* affirms the possibility of self-sufficiency by virtue of pantheistic dreams within a Heraclitean flux.

The third major kind of pastoral affirmation by Rousseau glorifies the *idylle en famille à la campagne,* and its most famous statement occurs in the seventh letter of the fifth part of *La Nouvelle Héloïse:* "On oublie son siecle et ses contemporains; on se transporte au tems des patriarches; on veut mettre soi-même la main à l'œuvre, partager les travaux rustiques, et le bonheur qu'on y voit attaché. O tems de l'amour et de l'innocence, où les femmes étoient tendres et modestes, où les hommes étoient simples et vivoient contens! O Rachel! fille charmante et si constamment aimée, heureux celui qui pour t'obtenir ne regretta pas quatorze ans d'esclavage! O douce élève de Noëmi, heureux le bon vieillard dont tu réchauffois les pieds et le cœur! Non, jamais la beauté ne regne avec plus d'empire qu'au milieu des soins champêtres. C'est là que les graces sont sur leur trône, que la simplicité les pare, que la gaité les anime, et qu'il faut les adorer malgré soi. Pardon, Milord, je reviens à nous" (II, 603, 4). Commenting on the background of this extraordinary letter, Bernard Guyon asserts: "L'auteur de ce texte n'est pas seulement un humaniste nourri des poètes antiques exaltant l'âge d'or . . . il est surtout un être profondément *religieux* et par sa culture, ses souvenirs d'enfance, ses lectures de la Bible, et par sa nature profonde. L'originalité de ce texte est là, marquée par le culte de Dionysos, discret mais très réel; par l'évocation des temps des Patriarches; plus profondément, par la découverte de réalités primitives, de rites antiques et universels . . ." (II, 1709).

Given the rarity of the theme of the "happy family" (in the Graeco-Roman and feudal world, the family unit fulfills mainly a political and social function, the most memorable exception being Hector's farewell to Andromache and Astyanax in the sixth book of the *Iliad*), it is not surprising that Rousseau, under the sway of the Calvinist tradition, should have drawn on the Bible to sustain his pastoral and personal dream of *le bonheur en famille.* It may well be that the finest biblical pastoral lines of nineteenth century French and English poetry bear some relation to Rousseau's apostrophe—I have, of course, in mind "Le rêve de Booz" and the "Ode to a Nightingale." To be sure, many of his descriptions in the fourth and fifth parts of *La Nouvelle Héloïse* evoke the "happy family" in a context devoid of biblical and poetic references. For the most part, these descriptions and ethical analyses are animated by Rousseau's conjugal imperatives: "Je veux aimer l'époux que tu [l'Etre] m'as donné. Je veux être fidele . . . Je veux être chaste . . ." (II, 357) as well as by his sociological and economic philosophy derived from his *Discours sur les sciences et les arts* and *Discours sur l'origine de l'inégalité.*

The historical and literary effects of Rousseau's modernization of the classical pastoral idyll have not yet been fully elucidated, although most essays related to Romanticism touch in one way or another upon aspects of the idyllic experience in the manner of Rousseau. For the sake of clarification, one should distinguish: 1. episodes in nineteenth and twentieth century literatures patterned on *l'Idylle des Cerises,* itself a reformulation of the classical idyll; 2. experiences of idyllic self-sufficiency derived from *l'Idylle des Charmettes* and *La cinquième rêverie du promeneur solitaire;* 3. episodes which evoke the family idyll based in part on scenes from *La Nouvelle Héloïse* and on scenes from *Les Confessions* (M. Lambercier and *les idylles à trois:* Rousseau and Mme de Warens and Claude Anet as well as Mme d'Houdetot and Lambert). With these three categories well in mind, one could study to what degree each of them has been *expanded, contracted,* or *integrated* into a context more or less alien to the mood of the traditional idyll. Furthermore, such an investigation would have to consider the treatment of idyllic episodes (genre, setting etc.). *Paul et Virginie,* for instance, illustrates colorfully and at length *les amours sans mystère* of its pastoral protagonists for whom "chaque jour . . . étoit un jour de fête . . .",[54] whereas Lamartine's *Jocelyn* portrays in pale and flowing alexandrines the chaste Jocelyn and Laurence in their pastoral grotto "épuisant le bonheur dans toute sa goutte de vie."[55] More rustic than Lamartine's endeavors and certainly more prosaic are, according to Cararra, "gli scritti della Sand."[56] Her preface to *François le Champi*—Marcel Proust's childhood favorite—reveals clearly that *Lélia* knew what was happening: ". . . voyons, le théâtre, la poésie et le roman ont quitté la houlette pour prendre le poignard, et quand ils mettent en scène la vie rustique, ils donnent un certain caractère de réalité qui manquait aux bergeries du temps passé. Mais la poésie n'y est guère, et je m'en plains . . ."[57]

A delightfully ironic example of idyllic contraction *en prose* may be found in chapter XII of *Le rouge et le noir* graced with the subtitle "Les bas à jour": "Jamais je n'accorderai rien à Julien, se dit Madame de Renâl, nous vivrons à l'avenir comme nous vivons depuis un mois. Ce sera un ami." Disregarding for the sake of brevity Madame de Mortsauf's idyllic *Vollglück in der Beschränkung,* we may surely interpret Balzac's beautiful evocation of his beloved Touraine as being an idyllic reflection of *l'Idylle des Charmettes:* "En ce moment, les moulins situés sur les chutes de l'Indre donnaient une voix à cette vallée frémissante, les peupliers se balançaient en riant, pas un nuage au ciel, les oiseaux chantaient, les cigales criaient, tout y était mélodie. Ne me demandez plus pourquoi j'aime la Touraine; je ne l'aime ni comme on aime son berceau, ni comme un artiste aime l'art; je l'aime moins que je ne vous aime; mais sans la Touraine, peut-être ne vivrais-je plus."[58] Likewise, Proust's meditations concerning a group of girls on the shores of Balbec are surely issued from *l'Idylle des Cerises,* and perhaps modified by Gérard de Nerval's *Sylvie*—meditations, integrated in a fresco, which like the *Confessions* unfold in the dimension of time: "Elles étaient, du bonheur inconnu et possible de la vie, un exemplaire si délicieux et en si parfait état, que c'était presque pour des raisons intellectuelles que j'étais désespéré de ne pas pouvoir faire dans des conditions uniques, ne laissant aucune place à l'erreur possible, l'expérience de ce que nous offre de plus mystérieux la beauté qu'on désire, et qu'on se console de ne posséder jamais en demandant du plaisir ..."[59]

Whether Proust's marine idyll could or should be related to Sannazaro's Latin mythological poem *Salices,* 1517, in which certain nymphs are pursued by certain satyrs, may be irrelevant to our line of inquiry. More pertinent is Camus' injunction in *L'homme révolté:* "Il faut détruire ceux qui détruisent l'idylle ..."[60] Admittedly his pagan celebrations in *Noces* and happy interludes in *L'étranger* seem too sensuous to qualify under the heading of *amour sans mystère et sans honte.* On second thought, and after comparing Camus' idylls to raptures by Gide, Giono and Montherlant, I feel that his artistic powers of *Beschränkung* are so intense that they somehow neutralize effects of carnal indulgence, creating an ideal of innocent and "shameless" love which for Camus is but a pretext for idyllic prose: "Nous marchons à la rencontre de l'amour et du désir. Nous ne cherchons pas de leçons, ni l'amère philosophie qu'on demande à la grandeur. Hors du soleil, des baisers et des parfums sauvages, tout nous paraît futile."[61]

Antithetical to Rousseau's *Idylle des Cerises* stand Sartre's and Beckett's anti-idylls acted out by Henri and Lulu and Molloy and Edith. Like Camus' Meursault, these characters have been sired by Dostoyevsky who, according to Poggioli, subverted the myth of the Golden Age by projecting the idyllic vision into a dream, turning that dream into a nightmare "to prove that the inner necessity of that ideal of perfection by which the revolutionary spirit tempts and threatens the human soul, turns it into its very opposite or into a corruption never dreamed before."[62] But a history of the modern idyll would also have to trace filiations between Rousseau's three categories of idylls and the German idyll variously characterized by *Familienglück oder -unglück* (from Voss' *Luise* praising the *pater familias* drinking coffee to Goethe's *Hermann und Dorothea* unto Hofmannsthal's *Idylle*). It is important to stress that most family idylls in the tradition of *Hermann und Dorothea* incorporate a polarity which we have seen to be characteristic of the classical pastoral (town vs. country, Age of Gold vs. Age of Iron, reality vs. unreality). But whereas the classical pastoral rejects the present in favor of a luminous past, *die bürgerliche Idylle* considers the *present* as being ideal, establishing the necessary polarity between it and the future dark with threats and doom:

> Alles regt sich, als wollte die Welt, die gestaltete, rückwärts
> Lösen in Chaos und Nacht sich auf und neu sich gestalten.[63]

The Goethean idyll is centered in the here and now, and while Goethe's Arcadian scene in *Faust* II and his poetic commentary on the *Wilhelm Tischbein Idylle* do not relate directly to the Rousseauean idylls under discussion, they nonetheless correspond in their intention to Rousseau's obsession to transform his intuition of the Golden Age into a happy fate. By analogy, Horst Rüdiger's remarkable analysis illuminates my point of view: "Doch während Tasso im *Aminta* wie in Goethes Drama ein *verlorenes* Paradies beklagt, sind Fausts Energien ganz auf gegenwärtige *Erfüllung* seiner Liebe zu Helena gerichtet: der in die graue Vorzeit verbannte Wunschtraum hat sich in "heiterstes Geschick" verwandelt, das Glück der Liebenden ist an die Stelle von Tassos Leiden getreten."[64]

A perfect artistic synthesis of Rousseau's three idyllic categories occurs in Kleist's letter to his sister Ulrike on May 1, 1802, about his stay on an island on the river Aar, near Thun in the canton of Berne. The analogy between Rousseau's three idylls under discussion and Kleist's *erlebtem idyllischen Glück* is so striking that the passage deserves to be quoted in its entirety:

Jetzt leb' ich auf einer Insel in der Aare, am Ausfluss des Thunersees, recht eingeschlossen von Alpen, 1/4 Meile von der Stadt. Ein kleines Häuschen an der Spitze, das wegen seiner Entlegenheit sehr wohlfeil war, habe ich für sechs Monate gemietet und bewohne es ganz allein. Auf der Insel wohnt auch weiter niemand, als nur an der andern Spitze eine kleine Fischerfamilie, mit der ich schon einmal um Mitternacht auf den See gefahren bin, wenn sie Netze einzieht und auswirft. Der Vater hat mir von zwei Töchtern eine in mein Haus gegeben, die mir die Wirthschaft führt: ein freundlich-liebes Mädchen, das sich ausnimmt, wie ihr Taufname: Mädeli. Mit der Sonne stehen wir auf, sie pflanzt mir Blumen in den Garten, bereitet mir die Küche, während ich arbeite für die Rückkehr zu Euch; dann essen wir zusammen; Sonntag zieht sie die schöne Schwyzertracht an, ein Geschenk von mir, wir schiffen uns über, sie geht in die Kirche nach Thun, ich besteige das Schreckhorn, und nach der Andacht kehren wir beide zurück. Weiter weiss ich von der ganzen Welt nichts mehr.[65]

Kleist blends the pastoral-erotic element of *l'Idylle des Cerises* with the Epicurean theme of *l'Idylle des Charmettes* (compare: "je me levois avec le soleil" to "Mit der Sonne stehen wir auf . . .") and even succeeds in relating to this synthesis the theme of the happy humble family—fishermen on an island not far in spirit and space from *l'Ile de Saint-Pierre* inhabited by "le Receveur avec sa famille . . ." (I, 1041).

Related to Rousseau's *bonheur idyllique*, but intensified and cast into a consciously artistic although exquisitely simple form, are the poems and prose passages of Eichendorff's romantic tale *Aus dem Leben eines Taugenichts* which evokes many a summer night reminiscent of Jean-Jacques' night beneath the stars: ". . . cette nuit délicieuse hors de la ville dans un chemin qui cotoyoit le Rhône ou la Saône . . ." (I, 168). Indeed, Renate Böschenstein is right when she affirms in her informative volume entitled *Idylle:* "Eichendorff ist derjenige romantische Dichter, der zur Idylle in der engsten Beziehung steht. Nicht nur, dass bei ihm die Idee der Idylle am häufigsten sichtbar wird; Eichendorff hat auch versucht, seine poetische Welt in einer Idylle zu kristallisieren."[66] Far more closely related to Jean-Jacques' idylls than Hebbel's "Mutter und Kind" and Mörike's poem "Der alte Turmhahn" are many idyllic chapters in Gottfried Keller's first part of *Der grüne Heinrich*, the so-called *Jugendgeschichte*. Either, as I shall try to show in the chapter on Rousseau and Keller, the latter transfigures thematic patterns bequeathed to him by his first love, Jean Paul, or transmutes episodes from the *Confessions* like, for instance, *l'Idylle des Cerises*, which is the basis of his chapter entitled "Judith" describing her climbing an apple tree and offering its fruit to Heinrich Lee. After Gottfried Keller the theme and treatment of the three idyllic motifs established by Rousseau become rare, and the melodic patterns of his oaten flute are drowned by Wagnerian orchestration and Nietzschean dissonances so common towards the end of the nineteenth and twentieth century German literature. Hesse, sometimes, remembers to be pure and simple. Thomas Mann, although imbued with the thought and ideology of Rousseau, disdains his simplicity and straightforwardness, and prefers to confront in the chapter "Schnee" of the *Zauberberg* an orthodox italianate pastoral scene with its destructive counterpart—the entire episode patterned obviously and awkwardly on Goethean and Dostoyevskian models. The idyll concludes, however, on a humanistic note: "Der Mensch soll um der Güte und Liebe willen dem Tode keine Herrschaft einräumen über seine Gedanken."[67]

Turning our attention to England, its literature of the late eighteenth century offers few idyllic analogues to our three categories under discussion. The English neo-classical pastoral tradition exemplified by Pope's *Pastorals*, 1704, is being challenged by the realistic influence of Goldsmith's *The Vicar of Wakefield*, stressing, as will later on Burns' "The Cotter's Saturday Night," 1786, the naturalistic family idyll. Equally far removed from Rousseau's attempt to modernize the idyll is Crabbe's "The Village," 1783:

> On Mincio's banks, in Caesar's bounteous reign,
> If Tityrus found the Golden Age again,
> Must sleepy bards the flattering dream prolong,
> Mechanic echoes of the Mantuan song.[68]

For Romantic analogues to Rousseau's three idyllic categories, I refer the reader to standard works by Henri Peyre, Henri Roddier, E. Leguis, H. Read, and above all, for the problem that concerns us, to Jacques Voisine's study of Rousseau's influence on the English Romantics[69]—an influence which was immense and which this essay does not even attempt to summarize. Byron never wrote in the manner of Jean-Jacques, and Shelley, although deeply influenced by him, rarely evokes simple, intimate, warm idylls. Keats, it seems, despised Rousseau. Wordsworth makes no mention of him whatsoever, and it took Hazlitt, inveterate *rousseauiste,* to remind critics how much and how little the author of the *Preludes* has in common with Jean-Jacques:

The writer who most nearly resembles him in our times is the author of the *Lyrical Ballads.* We see no other difference between them, than that the one wrote in prose and the other in poetry; and that prose is perhaps better adapted to express those local and personal feelings, which are inveterate habits in the mind, than poetry, which embodies its imaginary creations. We conceive that Rousseau's exclamation, 'Ah, voilà de la pervenche,' comes more home to the mind than Mr. Wordsworth's discovery of the linnet's nest 'with five blue eggs,' or than his address to the cuckoo, beautiful as we think it is; and we will confidently match the Citizen of Geneva's adventures on the Lake of Bienne against the Cumberland Poet's floating dreams on the Lake of Grasmere. Both create an interest out of nothing, or rather out of their own feelings; both weave numberless recollections into one sentiment; both wind their own being round whatever object occurs to them. But Rousseau, as a prose writer, gives only the habitual and personal impression. Mr. Wordsworth as a poet, is forced to lend the colours of imagination to impressions which owe all their force to their identity within themselves, and tries to paint what is only to be felt. Rousseau, in a word, interests you in certain objects by interesting you in himself: Mr. Wordsworth would persuade you that the most insignificant objects are interesting in themselves, because he is interested in them. If he had met with Rousseau's favorite periwinkle, he would have *translated* it into the most beautiful of flowers. This is not imagination, but want of sense. If his jealousy of the sympathy of others makes him avoid what is beautiful and grand in nature, why does he undertake elaborately to describe other objects? *His* nature is a mere Dulcinea del Toboso, and he would make a Vashti of her.[70]

Jacques Voisine has analyzed patiently and perspicaciously Rousseau's influence on Wordsworth's poetic revolution and devotes the most important chapter of his book to revealing the many affinities between Hazlitt and Rousseau—affinities that often dovetail viewpoints that I have tried to outline in this essay. The Victorians offer if not equivalents to, at least approximations of, Rousseau's idylls. One thinks of Meredith's *The Ordeal of Richard Feverel* where chapters XIV and XV respectively entitled "An Attraction" and "Ferdinand and Miranda" constitute a conglomerate of pastoral elements drawn from *The Tempest* and *l'Idylle des Cerises.* A chance meeting on a weir during which the hero, much like Jean-Jacques, steps from a boat into the water gives rise to this disquisition: "She was simply dressed, befitting decency

and the season. On a closer inspection you might see that her lips
were stained. This blooming young person was regaling on dewberries . . . Fastidious youth, which revolts at woman plumping
her exquisite proportions on bread-and-butter, and would (we
must suppose) joyfully have her scraggy to have her poetical, can
hardly object to dewberries. Indeed the act of eating them is
dainty and induces musing. The dewberry is a sister to the lotus,
and an innocent sister."[71] The point seems well taken in regard
to Tennyson who modifies pastoral and epicurean themes of *La
cinquième rêverie du promeneur solitaire* into nostalgic ecstasies
of his "Lotus Eaters."

> How sweet it were, hearing the downward stream,
> With half-shut eyes ever to seem
> Falling asleep in a half-dream!
> To dream and dream, like yonder amber light . . .

And while Jean-Jacques rises at dawn to see the sunrise and to live
that day *l'Idylle des Cerises,* Tennyson, haunted by the vision of
an artificial paradise, has his "Dream of the Fair Women":

> I knew the flowers, I knew the leaves, I knew
> The tearful glimmer of the languid dawn . . .

only to meet

> . . . a lady within call,
> Stiller than chiselled marble, standing there;
> A daughter of the gods, divinely tall,
> And most divinely fair.

Mlles Galley and Graffenried have turned to stone.

Far closer to Rousseau in his idyllic experience than either
Wordsworth or Tennyson is Henry David Thoreau, and because of
the importance of the relationship between the Citizen of Geneva
and the Citizen of Concord, I have devoted a separate chapter to
them.

Whereas Italian literature of the late eighteenth and early nineteenth century resounds with echoes of its pastoral tradition and
reminiscences of Gessner, not one Italian prose writer or poet
creates stylistic and thematic equivalent to Rousseau's idyll,
mainly because *formal* considerations—especially in Italy—were
too powerful to allow a simple and direct expression of *uno stato
d'animo.* What Hazlitt said concerning Rousseau and Wordsworth
applies indeed to most post-Romantic Rousseauean authors, and
it is worthwhile to quote once more Hazlitt to focus on the prob-

lem: ". . . Rousseau, as a prose writer, gives only the habitual and personal impression. Mr. Wordsworth, as a poet, is forced to lend the colours of imagination to impressions which owe all their force to their identity within themselves, and tries to paint what is only to be felt. Rousseau, in a word, interests you in certain objects by interesting you in himself: Mr. Wordsworth would persuade you that the most insignificant objects are interesting in themselves, because he is interested in them." What Hazlitt seems to be saying is that in the case of Rousseau, *le style est sa vie*. If this be true, it becomes understandable that Leopardi, the one Romantic poet whose purity reminds one of Rousseau's, could not in his *Idilli* recall a happy summer day spent with two girls or "sentir avec plaisir son existence, sans prendre la peine de penser" (I, 1045). To Leopardi, the surrender of his Ego to nature is always fraught with sadness:

> Così tra questa
> immensità s'annega il pensier mio:
> e il naufragar m'è dolce in questo mare. "L'infinito"

Still farther removed from Rousseau's idyllic strains are D'Annunzio's pastoral fable "La figlia di Jorio" and Carducci's well known "Idillio maremmano." As for twentieth century Italian writing, Ungaretti's and Montale's desire to overcome orthodox themes and rhythmic patterns, seconded by the influence of Apollinaire and others, is too strong not to vitiate any attempt to express simply personal idyllic experience.

It is also noteworthy that in Spain Rousseau's reformulation of the classical idyll into personal idylls such as *l'Idylle des Cerises* had little if any effect, since Gongora's reduction of the dialogued eclogues of Garcilaso and Herrera into *Soledades* precluded any major dramatic expansion of the genre. Furthermore, the hispanic tendency to divide autobiographical experience either into accounts of mystic journeys by sundry saints, or calvaries of pícaros, impeded the development in the late eighteenth and early nineteenth century of humanistic autobiographies like Rousseau's *Confessions*, Boswell's *Journals* or Goethe's *Dichtung und Wahrheit* out of which modern idylls could have issued. Spanish nineteenth century literature offers few if any analogues to Rousseau's idylls— neither Fernán Caballero's *La Gaviota* nor Valera's *Pepita Jiménez* contains idyllic themes comparable to Rousseau's. As for the theme of the Epicurean and Horatian "happy man", one may note the

Spanish propensity to mock him—*se burlan de los necios felices.* Whether fragments of Azorín's prose and poems by Jiménez, Lorca, Guillén, and Pedro Salinas embody Rousseau's idyllic moods is doubtful, since these poets experience states of being so intense that they revert to being reflections on being:

> soy, más estoy, Respiro.
> Lo profundo es el aire.
> La realidad me inventa
> Soy su leyenda ¡Salve![72]

Parallel to the development of the classical idyll as metamorphosed by Rousseau and defined by Jean Paul, there occurs at the end of the eighteenth and during the nineteenth and twentieth centuries of French literature, a renascence of hellenism which has been so closely studied by Professor Henri Peyre.[73] Its high points are Chénier's *Bucoliques,* Leconte de Lisle's *Poèmes antiques,* Guérin's *Centaure* and, above all, Mallarmé's *Après-midi d'un Faune.* Yet, despite the consciously Graeco-Roman nature of these idyllic evocations, the influence of Rousseau's *Idylles* and *Rêveries* can be detected in the last two works by virtue of their confessional mood which, although masked, animates *faune* and *centaure.* At the risk of courting paradox, which in a discussion of Rousseau may after all be unavoidable, I feel that Jean-Jacques' melodious, warm and serene style is closer to Theocritus' sense of form, his Greek melody and lightness of touch as well as his restraint and love of simple things, than is the slightly mannered formalism of Guérin and Mallarmé. "Or, l'essentiel, en littérature," writes Professor Peyre, "presque autant que dans d'autres arts, n'est pas toujours le contenu idéologique de l'œuvre, mais la forme, c'est-à-dire le ton, la chaleur, l'intensité prêtés à certaines pensées par une imagination puissante, une vive sensibilité, un style coloré ou musical."[74] With the advent of Rousseau—prophet of the new world—the true humanist no longer adorns his work with the details of classical learning, but structures it according to the essence of the classical experience itself, as for instance, Manet who conceives his *Déjeuner sur l'herbe* according to the composition of Giorgione's *Concert champêtre.*

One may, therefore, interpret Rousseau's *Idylle des Cerises* as a fortunate moment in a literary tradition which for want of a better term may be called *l'histoire du bonheur humain.*[75] It is a tradition admittedly problematical in nature, at the mercy of Jansenists, Hegelians, Freudians, and Marxists alike, and hardly comparable in size and importance to the overwhelmingly tragic and often sadistic implications of European literature. The pastoral genre, on the surface the least desperate of literary modes, by its very obsession with the Hesiodic dream of the Golden Age when men "lived in ease and peace upon their lands with many good things, rich in flocks and beloved of the blessed gods," insinuates doubts and questions that have never been raised more subtly than by Marvell:

> Thenceforth I set myself to play
> My solitary time away,
> With this; and very well content
> Could so mine idle Life have spent.
> For it was full of sport; and light
> Of foot, and heart; and did invite
> Me to its game: It seemed to bless
> Itself in me. How could I less
> Than love it?
>   "The Nymph complaining for the death of her faun"

And no pastoral poet ever responded more movingly to this reproach than did Jean-Jacques Rousseau when he said: "La soif du bonheur ne s'éteint point dans le cœur de l'homme . . ." (I, 413). Could it be that in living as well as writing *l'Idylle des Cerises* he succeeded in quenching that thirst?

CHAPTER III

Rousseau's *La Nouvelle Héloïse* and Goethe's *Wilhelm Meisters Lehrjahre*

> Entraînés par la nature et par les hommes dans des routes contraires, forcés de nous partager entre ces diverses impulsions, nous en suivons une composée qui ne nous mène ni à l'un ni à l'autre but. Ainsi combattus et flottants durant tout le cours de notre vie, nous la terminons sans avoir pu nous accorder avec nous et sans avoir été bons ni pour nous, ni pour les autres (*Emile*).

> Ich bin gebildet genug, versetzte sie, um zu lieben und zu trauern (Mignon).

The sense of this essay is to compare these novels in the light of the concept of the *Bildungsroman*. Historians of literature have tended to restrict the use of this term to German literature, and Stammler speaks for many when he asserts: "Der Bildungsroman ist in gleicher Zielstrebigkeit in keiner anderen europäischen Literatur in so starkem Masse vertreten und kann als die deutsche Grossform des Romans überhaupt betrachtet werden."[1] If this be true, then *Wilhelm Meisters Lehrjahre, Bildungsroman par excellence,* should provide *comparatistes* with a convenient measure for assessing to what degree other masterpieces of French, Spanish, Italian, Russian and Anglo-American fiction may be regarded as *Bildungsromane.* Such comparisons, on the whole, have been disappointing; for example, a distinguished editor like Trunz concludes the *literaturgeschichtliche Stellung* of *Wilhelm Meisters Lehrjahre* by situating it in a frame of reference that includes Fielding's *Tom Jones* and Stendhal's *La Chartreuse de Parme* and excludes Rousseau's *La Nouvelle Héloïse* (VII, 627). This oversight is not only shocking because German scholarship devoted to the Enlightenment and Romanticism never fails to bring up the name of Rousseau, but also because in terms of Trunz' analysis, *La Nouvelle Héloïse* almost begs for comparison with *Wilhelm Meisters Lehrjahre:* "Die *Lehrjahre* sind nicht nur die Entwicklungsgeschichte eines jungen Mannes, sondern insofern er den Bildungsmächten seiner Zeit begegnet, sind sie eine ganze Bildungsgeschichte des 18. Jahrhunderts" (VII, 623). Goethe may have well stated the reason for this oversight when he has Lothario exclaim: ". . . [es] ist ein Hauptfehler gebildeter Menschen, dass sie alles an eine Idee, wenig oder nichts an einen Gegenstand wenden mögen" (VII, 431). In other words, the concept of the *Bildungsroman* that emerged from the analyses of Schiller, Dilthey, Gerhardt and others, has blinded critics as to the nature of the *Gegenstand,* that is, the novel viewed objectively. Once the *Begriff* began to take the place of the *Gegenstand,* i.e., the living novel in the Forsterian sense of the word, these critics were unable to realize that the *Bildungsroman* as such, not their concept of it, is a far more European phenomenon than they had imagined.

German critics have disregarded, therefore, the historical importance of *La Nouvelle Héloïse* in their discussion of the development of the *Bildungsroman.* The first one to compare Rousseau's and Goethe's literary achievements was Erich Schmidt who restricted the influence of *La Nouvelle Héloïse* to *Werther,* tracing a literary lineage from which few if any critics have deviated. Contemptuous of the second part, he shows little patience with its heroine: "Julie ist eine ganz andere geworden. Auf jeder Seite wird von ihrer Tugend geredet . . ."[2] and adds: "Bei Rousseau verläuft das Ganze im Sande . . ." Stubbornly interpreting the novel as a *Liebesroman,* he concludes: "Moses Mendelssohn allerdings, dem das Organ zum Verständnis der Liebesglut fehlte, konnte aussprechen, das einzige Gute an der Neuen Heloise seien die Excurse, und fragen, warum Rousseau nicht das poetische Beiwerk unterdrückt und lieber einen Band gesammelter Abhandlungen geliefert habe?"[3] Max Wundt elaborates Schmidt's prejudice: "Diese Gattung des sentimentalen Romans hat Rousseau geschaffen in den beiden ersten Teilen der Neuen Heloise, von denen ein glühendes inneres Leben ausströmt . . . Aber Rousseau wagte nicht die Konsequenzen zu ziehen, die zu einer tragischen Lösung drängten . . . Auch er wollte Moral predigen so gut wie Richardson, und so schrieb er die folgenden Teile, in denen die Moral der Gesellschaft über die Rechte des Herzens triumphiert. So hat erst Goethe diese Form zur Vollendung gebracht; die Leiden des jungen Werthers stehen ganz auf dieser Linie und führen sie zu ihrem Gipfel empor."[4] Less rigid than either Schmidt or Wundt, Dilthey nonetheless restates their arguments and offers his well known definition of the *Bildungsroman:* "Ich möchte die Romane, welche die Schule des Wilhelm Meisters ausmachen (denn Rousseaus verwandte Kunstform wirkte auf sie nicht fort), Bildungsromane nennen. Goethes Werk zeigt menschliche Ausbildung in verschiedenen Stufen, Gestalten, Lebensepochen."[5] Equally decisive in shaping later views is his definition of the *Bildungsroman:* "Der Hyperion gehört zu den Bildungsromanen, die unter dem Einfluss Rousseaus in Deutschland aus der Richtung unseres damaligen Geistes auf innere Kultur hervorgegangen sind. Unter ihnen haben nach Goethe und Jean Paul der Sternbald Tiecks, der Ofterdingen von Novalis und Hölderlins Hyperion eine dauernde literarische Geltung behauptet. Von dem Wilhelm Meister und dem Hesperus ab stellen sie alle den Jüngling jener Tage dar; wie er in glücklicher Dämmerung in das Leben eintritt, nach verwandten Seelen sucht, der Freundschaft begegnet und der Liebe, wie er nun aber mit den harten Realitäten der Welt in Kampf gerät und so unter mannigfachen Lebenserfahrung heranreift, sich selber findet und seiner Aufgabe in der Welt gewiss wird. Die Aufgabe Goethes war die Geschichte eines sich zur Tätigkeit bildenden Menschen, das Thema beider Romantiker war der Dichter; Hölderlins Held war die heroische Natur welche ins Ganze zu wirken strebt und sich schliesslich doch in ihr eigenes Denken und Dichten zurückgeworfen findet."[6] In the same book, Dilthey devotes a long paragraph to retelling Rousseau's account in his *Confessions* of the genesis of *La Nouvelle Héloïse,* insisting solely on Rousseau's inability to observe human beings—Rousseau, whom Kant considered the Newton of the moral world! "In dem neueren Europa schuf zuerst Jean Jacques Rousseau in der neuen Heloise ein siegreich wirkendes Kunstwerk auf dem Weg einer Entfaltung von Gestalten aus dem Reichtum eigenen inneren Erlebens und Denkens, ohne eine hervorragende Begabung oder Gewöhnung zur Wahrnehmung oder Beobachtung anderer Menschen und ihrer Zustände. Durch das unselige Leben dieses mächtigen Mannes geht die Unfähigkeit, irgendeinen Menschen in seinem wahrem Wesen zu erfassen."[7]

Equally misleading are the views propounded by Melitta Gerhard. Convinced that *La Nouvelle Héloïse* is but a novel about love and passion, this historian of the *Bildungsroman* denies that

Rousseau's novel has exerted any influence; and it is worthwhile
to quote her remarks which, like Dilthey's, have become exemplary
of later interpretations: "Haftet der Darstellung von Liebesschmer-
zen und -Entzückungen in diesen Werken zumeist etwas Künst-
liches an [the reference aims at the *romans galants* of the 17th
century], so gewinnt dann, besonders zuerst im französischen
Roman, mehr und mehr echtes Empfinden darin Ausdruck, und
es ist bei aller Neuartigkeit und aller Bedeutung eines schöp-
ferischen Ereignisses doch nur der Durchbruch eines längst vor-
bereiteten Prozesses, wenn Rousseau 'Nouvelle Héloïse' schliesslich
den Weg zur unmittelbaren Aussprache und Analyse der Leiden-
schaft im Roman findet."[8] Her exposition concludes as follows:
"Vor Wilhelm Meister liegt ein Chaos, das der Gestaltung zu
neuem Kosmos harrt. Und das ist die tiefste und einschneidende
Bedeutung von Goethes 'Wilhelm Meister', die erst Umfang und
Dauer seiner Nachwirkung erklärt: zum erstenmal ist hier aus
dieser neugeschaffenen Lage heraus der seelische Weg des Einzel-
nen gestaltet, hat die grosse Lebensfrage, vor die von jetzt an der
Mensch gestellt ist, künstlerischen Ausdruck gefunden . . ."[9] And
elsewhere: "Erst 'Wilhelm Meister' wird zum Muster einer Tradition."[10]

No less faithful to the tradition established by Schmidt, Borcherdt's important *Der Roman der Goethezeit* devotes its introduction and opening pages to *La Nouvelle Héloïse*, "Wendepunkt
in der europäischen Dichtungsentwicklung" only to affirm in 1949
well after the Flaubertian tradition and in the shadow of the
World War that the form and essence of the novel demand a hero:
"Die Realität des Romans verlangt dagegen einen Helden, der
in seinen menschlichen Schwächen und Krisen des Lebens uns zu
packen vermag. Die Aufklärung hatte durch ihre ethischen Postu-
late ein neues Ideal vom Menschen aufgestellt, das im Grunde nur
Ersatz für das christliche bot. Die Figuren beim Richardson, die
Pamela und der Grandison, Gellerts Gestalten, Wielands Agathon
sind Stufen in der Entwicklung dieses ethischen "Helden"-Ideals,
das immer auf eine Geradlinigkeit, auf eine höchste Zielsetzung
hinarbeitet, die von der des Heiligen nur durch den Mangel an
Transzendenz verschieden ist. Bei Rousseau dagegen verliert der
Begriff des "Helden" seinen Sinn. Die Menschen werden in ihrem
Sosein begriffen . . ."[11] Borcherdt concludes his exposition of *La
Nouvelle Héloïse* on a note as authoritarian as it is false: "In der

Tat wird man der historischen Bedeutung des Werkes nur gerecht, wenn man sich auf den *ersten Teil* begrenzt" (author's italics).[12]

To the best of my knowledge, only three critics have ever made a direct connection between *La Nouvelle Héloïse* and *Wilhelm Meister*. The first, E. Buss, states in a short article in *Die Allgemeine Deutsche Lehrerzeitung*, 1912: "Wenn Goethe in seinem *Wilhelm Meister* oft den Gang der Handlung durch Erörterungen über Kunst, Literatur, Theater usw. unterbricht, so scheint er Rousseaus Darstellungsweise zu folgen."[13] The other is Edmond Vermeil whose long essay is rich in insights: "W. Meister commence, en effet, par une crise sentimentale, songe au suicide, puis triomphe de cette crise en risquant sa personalité tout entière dans les épreuves que lui ménage le destin. L'idée d'épreuve est commune à Rousseau et à Goethe. Comme Saint-Preux, W. Meister se guérit de toute absorbante sentimentalité, de tout dilettantisme, pour s'élever à la connaissance des hommes, à la maîtrise de soi, à la pratique d'une profession déterminée et l'on sait quelle ampleur prend chez Goethe, le thème du voyage. Une comparaison détaillée que je ne puis entreprendre ici, mettrait aisément en évidence les motifs communs, montrerait aussi les enrichissements inouïs qu'apporte ici le génie de Goethe."[14] The third critic, Jacques Voisine, suggests in his discussions of the relationship between Rousseau and Goethe and Rousseau and Wordsworth the influence of the former on the authors of early 19th century *Bildungsromane*.[15]

To achieve such a comparison it is necessary to view the two novels without any preconceived notions of what a *Bildungsroman* ought to be, and the best point of departure for such an investigation is surely Schiller's criticism, since it reflects ideas contemporary with the inception of *Wilhelm Meister* and even modified to some extent Goethe's revision of its first draft. On having received the eighth and last book of *Wilhelm Meister,* Schiller wrote to Goethe on July 8, 1796: "Der Roman, so wie er da ist, nähert sich in mehreren Stücken der Epopöe, unter andern auch darin, dass er Maschinen hat, die in gewissem Sinne die Götter oder das regierende Schicksal darin vorstellen. Der Gegenstand forderte dieses. Meisters Lehrjahre sind keine bloss blinde Wirkung der Natur, sie sind eine Art von Experiment. Ein verborgen wirkender höherer Verstand, die Mächte des Turms, begleiten ihn mit ihrer Aufmerksamkeit, und ohne die Natur in ihrem freien Gange zu stören, beobachten, leiten sie ihn von ferne und zu einem Zwecke, davon er selbst keine Ahnung hat, noch haben darf" (VIII, 539). And after having understood the sense of Goethe's innovative technique of remote guidance control, Schiller continues his analysis by considering the notion of the *Lehrjahre* as such and its correlative of *Meisterschaft:* "Nun kann aber diese Idee der Meisterschaft, die nur das Werk der gereiften und vollendeten Erfahrung ist, den Helden des Romans nicht selbst leiten; sie kann und darf nicht als sein Zweck und sein Ziel vor ihm stehen; denn sobald er sich das Ziel dächte, so hätte er es *eo ipso* auch erreicht; sie muss also als Führerin *hinter* ihm stehen. Auf diese Art erhält das Ganze eine schöne Zweckmässigkeit, ohne dass der Held einen Zweck hätte; der Verstand findet also ein Geschäft ausgeführt, indes die Einbildungskraft völlig ihre Freiheit behauptet." (VIII, 540).

Wilhelm Meisters Lehrjahre centers attention on Wilhelm, the hero, viewed by an omniscient and ironic narrator whereas *La Nouvelle Héloïse* grants equal important to Saint-Preux and Julie. Its epistolary form precludes intervention by the author save by way of footnotes. *Chacun écrit pour soi,* reveals only what he or she feels, thinks, and experiences, not unlike a Jamesian "reflector." Despite lengthy digressions, *La Nouvelle Héloïse* creates an impression of concentration in the tradition of French classicism in that the lives of Julie, Claire, Saint-Preux, and Wolmar intersect and modify each other. Little happens, much is felt, and still more, thought. In the words of Marcel Raymond: "Tout se passe comme si l'auteur avait entendu suivre les préceptes de style et de composition de l'art classique de XVIIe siècle (c'est la leçon qu'il a apprise). Mais on n'écrit pas les livres qu'on veut!" (II, xvii). Rousseau was fully aware of his innovations in fictional narrative: "La chose qu'on y a le moins vue et qui en fera toujours un ouvrage unique est la simplicité du sujet et la chaine de l'intérest qui concentré entre trois personnes se soutient durant six volumes sans épisode, sans avanture romanesque, sans méchanceté d'aucune espéce, ni dans les personnages, ni dans les actions" (I, 546). The characters, extraordinarily independent of their author, evoke themselves richly, deeply, completely, in a manner that prefigures Joyce, Virginia Woolf, and, of course, Proust. Julie, especially, possesses the indefinable yet real presence of a woman, *toute femme* and, at the same time, *toute conscience.* Endowed with the autonomous power of the living, Rousseau's main characters do not need their readers to the same degree as do characters whose function

it is to present ideas or to gratify more or less childish fantasies—
in the words of Schopenhauer, "werklose Gaukeleien der Phantasie."[16] To a reader not interested in *das Leben an sich*, *La
Nouvelle Héloïse* is a boring novel.[17] Schopenhauer, it should be
added, has a clear view of the future of the novel and links *La
Nouvelle Héloïse* and *Wilhelm Meister:* "Ein Roman wird desto
höherer and edlerer Art sein, je mehr *inneres* und je weniger
äusseres Leben er darstellt; und dies Verhältnis wird als charak-
terisches Zeichen alle Abstufungen des Romans begleiten, vom
'Tristam Shandy' an bis zum rohesten und tatenreichsten Ritter-
oder Räuberroman herab. 'Tristam Shandy' freilich hat sogut wie
gar keine Handlung; aber wie sehr wenig hat die 'Neue Heloise'
und der 'Wilhelm Meister! Sogar 'Don Quijote' hat verhältnis-
mässig wenig, besonders aber sehr unbedeutende, auf Scherz
hinauslaufende Handlung: und diese vier Romane sind die Krone
der Gattung."[18]

Whereas in Rousseau's *Bildungsroman* tensions mount and sub-
side exclusively between the characters, in Goethe's novel dramatic
tension is, generally speaking, restricted to manifesting itself in
oscillations between the hero and the narrator's powerful mind
and becomes the source, as in *La Chartreuse de Parme,* of lucid
and charmingly ironic effects that do not invalidate serious inten-
tions—in the words of Friedrich Schlegel: "Man lasse sich also
dadurch, dass der Dichter selbst die Personen und die Begeben-
heiten so leicht und so launig zu nehmen, den Helden fast nie
ohne Ironie zu erwähnen und auf sein Meisterwerk selbst von der
Höhe seines Geistes herabzulächeln scheint, nicht täuschen, als sei
es ihm nicht der heiligste Ernst" (VIII, 559). Wilhelm's apprenticeship develops through journeys, fleeting acquaintances with realistic, allegorical, and mythical representatives of mankind, and
above all through the effects of a concatenation of fate, will,
reason, and instinct. Mystery plays a major role in the overt
manifestations of the plot and expresses according to Victor Lange
"Goethe's wish to represent symbolically the ambiguous and uncertain forces that determine Wilhelm's actions and that slowly
illuminate his understanding."[19] Unquestionably this statement
applies to Rousseau as well, since he, like Goethe, seeks to evoke
the growth of a youth, and above all, of *an ethos which is to some
extent generated by the hero himself* and, at the same time, influenced by fate, advice, and circumstances. The main tension in
Wilhelm Meister being between Goethe's mind on the one hand,

and Wilhelm and his companions on the other, it becomes understandable that his hero should appear quite passive, and Goethe's famous comments in the seventh chapter of the fifth book justify this passivity: "Der Romanheld muss leidend, wenigstens nicht im hohen Grade wirkend sein . . ." (VII, 307). And Goethe continues his analysis by asserting "dass man dem Zufall im Roman gar wohl sein Spiel erlauben könne, dass er aber immer durch die Gesinnungen der Personen gelenkt und geleitet werden müsse . . ." (VII, 308). It is worthwhile to note that Saint-Preux' character is perhaps more passive than Wilhelm's, but that as far as his relation to his author is concerned, Saint-Preux, as I have tried to suggest, enjoys far more independence than his German counterpart.

"Sors de l'enfance, ami, reveille-toi," Mylord Edouard admonishes Saint-Preux in quasi Homerian terms.[20] "Ne livre point ta vie entiere au long sommeil de la raison. L'âge s'écoule, il ne t'en reste plus que pour être sage. A trente ans passés, il est temps de songer à soi; commence donc à rentrer en toi-même, et sois homme une fois avant la mort" (II, 523). In a similar vein, Lothario addresses himself to Wilhelm: "Man ist nicht immer Jüngling, und man sollte nicht immer Kind sein" (VII, 467). His advice coincides with Wilhelm's deepest aspiration: ". . . mich selbst, ganz wie ich da bin, auszubilden, das war dunkel von Jugend auf mein Wunsch und meine Absicht" (VII, 290). Parallel to the *Confessions* and the *Emile, La Nouvelle Héloïse* proclaims the view that a man must fulfill his potential: "Mes enfans, nous dit-il d'un ton d'autant plus touchant qu'il partoit d'un homme tranquille; soyez ce que vous êtes, et nous serons tous contens" (II, 496). Madame Wolmar echoes her husband and casts her injunctions in almost Kantian terms: ". . . je ne serai jamais contente de vous et de moi, que quand vous serez en effet tel que vous devez être, et que vous aimerez les devoirs que vous avez à remplir" (II, 670).

Both Saint-Preux and Wilhelm belong to the middle-class and both suffer from class-distinctions. The latter envies aristocrats and contemplates a *Missheirat:* "Dreimal glücklich sind diejenigen zu preisen, die ihre Geburt sogleich über die untern Stufen der Menschheit hinaushebt . . ." (VII, 154). Saint-Preux, "un Quidam sans azile, et réduit à vivre d'aumônes . . ." (II, 169) foreshadows Werther poor and humiliated, and his cry "Mais moi, Julie, hélas! errant, sans famille, et presque sans patrie, je n'ai que vous sur la terre, et l'amour seul me tient lieu de tout." (II, 73) summarizes aspects of Werther's existential loneliness. It is precisely because of the resemblance between Saint-Preux of the first part of *La Nouvelle Héloïse* and Werther, that German critics have restricted the influence of Rousseau's novel to *Die Leiden des jungen Werther*. "Discounting" Philine, Wilhelm loves four women: Marianne, the countess, Therese, and Natalie, the latter being according to Schlechta "das ideale", the former "das empirische Weib."[21] Saint-Preux, of course, devotes himself exclusively to Julie who embodies, it would seem, Marianne's passion, Therese's good sense, and Natalie's virtue as well as certain pietistic tendencies of *die schöne Seele*. Is she not called *une belle âme?* And do not Claire's admonishments find their echo in Goethe's novel which criticizes the inactive nature of pietism?: "Ta douceur, ta dévotion t'ont donné du penchant à l'humilité. Défie-toi de cette dangereuse vertu qui ne fait qu'animer l'amour-propre en le concentrant . . ." (II, 500). Unlike Natalie, who performs an almost allegorical function, Julie, very much alive, counterbalances ideally Saint-Preux' psychic presence. It is she who calls him to her arms where, owing to her love of him, he will at last find himself, unified and at peace with himself: "Vien donc, ame de mon cœur, vie de ma vie, vien te réunir à toi-même . . ." (II, 146).

Given Rousseau's epistolary form, it is imperative that each major character have a sense of time that reveals his past in relation to the events in the novel.[22] Each character grows old, and many of their temporal experiences foreshadow those of Proust. The theme of *le temps vécu* absorbs much of their thoughts and feelings: "Ainsi nous recommençons de vivre pour recommencer de souffrir, et le sentiment de notre existence n'est pour nous qu'un sentiment de douleur. Infortunés! Que sommes-nous devenus? Comment avons-nous cessé d'être ce que nous fumes?" (II, 336). On the whole, Wilhelm knows little *Daseinsnot,* since Goethe tends to assign excessive feelings to specific characters whose functions seem, at times, almost allegorical or symbolic. For example, the Harfner exemplifies the dread of nothingness: ". . . bloss in sich gekehrt, betrachtete er sein hohles, leeres Ich, das ihm als ein unermesslicher Abgrund erschien." (VII, 436). Similarly, Aurelie illustrates the sufferings of the schizophrenic mind: ". . . mein Freund, mein Vertrauter, welche entsetzliche Arbeit ist es, sich mit Gewalt von sich selbst zu entfernen!" (VII, 279). In other words, the feelings and experiences in *Wilhelm Meister* and *La Nouvelle*

Héloïse are often the same, but the demands of the *form* of the two novels cast the *Erlebnisse* into different kinds of characters and even different poetic genres. It is well known that Goethe had misgivings about the novel's being a pure art form. Hence, he reserves the expression of certain emotional states to poetry alone:

> Wer nie sein Brot mit Tränen ass,
> Wer nie die kummervollen Nächte
> Auf seinem Bette weinend sass,
> Der kennt Euch nicht, ihr himmlischen Mächte.
>
> Ihr führt ins Leben uns hinein,
> Ihr lasst den Armen schuldig werden,
> Dann überlasst ihr ihn der Pein,
> Denn alle Schuld rächt sich auf Erden.

On hearing the Harfner's song, Wilhelm insists that these are *his* feelings: ". . . alles, was in meinem Herzen stockte, hast Du losgelöst . . ." (VII, 137). Likewise, Mignon, aside from her specifically "demonic" role, represents an integral aspect of Wilhelm's psyche: "Mein Kind! rief er aus, mein Kind! Du bist ja mein! Wenn Dich das Wort trösten kann. Du bist mein!" (VII, 143). Rousseau, instead of making separate use of poetry and prose as does Goethe, attempts to fuse the narrative and poetico-lyrical strains, creating hereby a new genre which may be designated as *le roman poème*. Admittedly, many sections of *La Nouvelle Héloïse* are didactic and descriptive. Yet, the following passage bears a remarkable likeness in terms of affect and theme to the Harfner's lament: "Ce n'est point le présent que je crains; c'est le passé qui me tourmente. Il est des souvenirs aussi redoutables que le sentiment actuel; on s'attendrit par reminiscence; on a honte de se sentir pleurer, et l'on n'en pleure que davantage. Ces larmes sont de pitié, de regret, de repentir; l'amour n'y a plus de part . . ." (II, 402, 3). Tears, regrets, and repentance sustain both the poem and the prose passage; the mood is the same. It is noteworthy that the Rousseauean fusion of the lyrical and the narrative modes so characteristic of *La Nouvelle Héloïse* had, in conjunction with the lyrical strain in the *Confessions,* a lasting influence on the lyrical *Bildungsroman,* be it Hölderlin's *Hyperion* or Novalis' *Heinrich von Ofterdingen,* supposedly an anti-Meister novel.

"Mais que faire aujourd'hui? Comment m'y prendre? Vous m'avez promis de l'amitié; voyez mes perplexités, et conseillez-moi" (II, 31). This second sentence of *La Nouvelle Héloïse* is of the very essence of the *Bildungsroman* which grants an essential role to the advisor and equal importance to his advice. "Par pitié," cries out Saint-Preux, "ne m'abandonnez pas à moi-même; daignez au moins disposer de mon sort . . ." (II, 35). His willingness to be led and to accept counsel has surprised French readers no longer raised on Fénelon's *Télémaque;* German readers, however, accustomed to the presence of pedagogues in fiction from Archytas (*Agathon*), the Abbé, to Settembrini in his threadbare coat and checkered trousers, consider such attitudes quite normal: Saint-Preux is as obedient a lover as he is a student: "Quoi-que vous puissiez me prescrire, je ne saurai qu'obéir. M'imposez-vous un silence éternel? je saurai me contraindre à le garder. Me bannissez-vous de votre présence? Je jure que vous ne me verrez plus" (II, 35). He welcomes paternal counsel from the husband of the woman he loves, much like Hans Castorp from Mynheer Peeperkorn ". . . il me parla comme un pere à son enfant, et me mit à force d'estime dans l'impossibilité de la [sa droiture] démentir" (II, 423). Goethe's hero, too, seeks, and welcomes advice and surrenders himself to friends and guides: " 'Ich überlasse mich ganz meinen Freunden und ihrer Führung,' sagte Wilhelm; 'es ist vergebens, in dieser Welt nach eigenem Willen zu streben' " (VII, 594).

Who are these mentors? Foremost, they are superior beings: "Voila ce qui doit arriver à toutes les ames d'une certaine trempe; elles transforment pour ainsi dire les autres en elles-mêmes; elles ont une sphère d'activité dans laquelle rien ne leur resiste . . ." (II, 204). Lothario elaborates the same idea: "Unglaublich ist es, was ein gebildeter Mensch für sich und andere tun kann, wenn er, ohne herrschen zu wollen, das Gemüt hat, Vormund von vielen zu sein, sie leitet, dasjenige zur rechten Zeit zu tun, was sie doch alle gerne tun möchten, und sie zu ihren Zwecken führt, die sie meist recht gut im Auge haben und nur die Wege dazu verfehlen" (VII, 608). The most important influence in Saint-Preux' life is Julie, *la prêcheuse,* who like Natalie, loves her charge and insists on complete obedience: "Pour moi, plus je m'occupe de notre situation, plus je trouve que la raison vous demande ce que je vous demande au nom de l'amour. Soyez donc docile à sa douce voix, et laissez-vous conduire, hélas, par une autre aveugle . . ." (II, 56). Both women seek to purify and to ennoble instinctive drives. Commenting on the manuscript of *die schöne Seele,* Natalie remarks to Wilhelm: "Jeder gebildete Mensch weiss, wie sehr er an sich und andern mit einer gewissen Roheit zu kämpfen hat, wieviel ihn seine Bildung kostet, und wie sehr er doch in gewissen Fällen nur an sich selbst denkt und vergisst, was er andern schuldig ist" (VII, 518). Julie's admonitions know no end. Her loving reply to Saint-Preux' admission to having spent a night "chez la femme d'un colonel" (II, 273) states truths that approximate Goethean attitudes: "Ignorez-vous qu'il y a des objets si odieux qu'il n'est pas même permis à l'homme d'honneur de les voir, et que l'indignation de la vertu ne peut supporter le spectacle du vice? Le sage observe le desordre public qu'il ne peut arrêter; il l'observe, et montre sur son visage attristé la douleur qu'il lui cause . . ." (II, 301). Whereas Rousseau assigns to his heroine sundry pedagogical functions (aside from lecturing on love with disquisitions on *le péché d'Onan,* she holds forth on virtue, marriage, religion, God, etc.), Goethe, true to his novelistic method, analyzes *den bildenden Einfluss der Frau* by submitting his hero to the influence of Philine, old Barbara, Mignon, Aurelie, Therese, and of course, Natalie.

The pedagogical role of men is equally powerful and often mysterious, much like the Ways of Providence. M. de Wolmar has methods of his own: ". . . je te jure," cries out Madame de Wolmar, "qu'il a quelque don surnaturel pour lire au fond des cœurs . . ." (II, 496). His passion is to understand and see: "Si je pouvois changer la nature de mon être et devenir un œil vivant, je ferois volontiers cet échange" (II, 491). His invitations are irresistible: "M. de Wolmar veut vous voir, il vous offre sa maison, son amitié, ses conseils . . ." (II, 417). Furthermore, like God, he knows best: "Mes enfans," he exclaims, addressing himself to his wife and her transcendental lover, ". . . je vous connois tous deux mieux que vous ne me connaissez . . ." (II, 490). Like M. de Wolmar and Mylord Edouard in the case of Saint-Preux, the Abbé, Jarno, Lothario, and the doctor, ". . . derselbe kleine tätige Mann . . . denn wir schon kennen . . ." (VII, 520), shape overtly and covertly the life of Wilhelm. Extensions of destiny, these agents move on the periphery of the drama and interfere at crucial moments in order to awaken latent energies and knowledge. "Enfin le voile est déchiré;" writes Saint-Preux to Madame d'Orbe, "cette longue illusion s'est évanouïe . . ." (II, 317). The notion of a necessary and beneficial process of self-deception is a key concept of the *Bildungsroman.* Saint-Preux' attitude towards Julie is a case in point. In love with the memory of Julie, who is no longer what she was, Saint-Preux is not allowed to realize that his love is "dated." "Otez-lui la mémoire, il n'aura plus d'amour" (II, 509). And M. de

Wolmar goes on to explain the nature of Saint-Preux' "creative" error: "L'erreur qui l'abuse et le trouble est de confondre les tems et de se reprocher souvent comme un sentiment actuel, ce qui n'est que l'effet d'un souvenir trop tendre; mais je ne sais s'il ne vaut pas mieux achever de le guérir que le desabuser. On tirera peut-être meilleur parti pour cela de son erreur, que de ses lumieres. Lui découvrir le véritable état de son cœur seroit lui apprendre la mort de ce qu'il aime . . ." (II, 510). Likewise, Wilhelm reappraises his life in terms of errors: "Leider hab' ich, 'versetzte Wilhelm,' nichts zu erzählen als Irrtümer, Verirrungen auf Verirrungen . . ." (VII, 446).

The ninth chapter of the seventh book of the *Lehrjahre* appears, at times, like a summary of the *Emile* whose principles in turn are applied in *La Nouvelle Héloïse*. The Abbé, related seemingly to both Fénelon and Goethe, also bears a strong resemblance to M. de Wolmar: "Mit einem heitern Gesicht und einem würdigen Ausdruck fing der Mann an: 'Nicht vor Irrtum zu bewahren, ist die Pflicht des Menschenerziehers, sondern den Irrenden zu leiten, ja ihn seinen Irrtum aus vollen Bechern ausschlürfen zu lassen, das ist Weisheit der Lehrer' " (VII, 494, 5).

Thus, error and illusion represent essential parts of the plot of both novels. This rift between appearance and reality generates ironic effects which, more obvious in *Wilhelm Meisters Lehrjahre,* are also felt in *La Nouvelle Héloïse*. Deeply convinced at the out-set of the novel of his undying devotion to Julie, Saint-Preux suffers in his heart of hearts a sense of inadequacy in love. His first comment to her about their night of love suggests a sense of failure:" . . . tu sais mieux aimer que moi" (II, 149). Indeed, it is possible to interpret Julie's willful marriage to M. de Wolmar as representing *un coup de grâce* for Saint-Preux behind whom lurks, after all, Jean-Jacques, who preferred adoration from afar to the task of sustained possession. In such a light, the famous cry: "O Julie, que c'est un fatal présent du ciel qu'une ame sensible!" (II, 89) assumes ambiguous meaning and stresses the venerable opposition between heart and reason, characteristic of both novels: "Die Vernunft ist grausam . . . das Herz ist besser" (VII, 489).

Led and stumbling through life, the two novices reach some in-sight into their respective dilemmas not unlike a patient under analysis. "Il est tems de devenir sage." (II, 375) admonishes Julie, "Il est tems que l'illusion cesse; il est tems de revenir d'un trop long égarement" (II, 376). Both heroes reconsider the roles that they intended to play: Saint-Preux that of lover, Wilhelm that of director of a theater. Their ambitions suffer from the same weakness: they are undefined. "Pour suivre son talent il le faut connoitre" (II, 537) sighs Saint-Preux and adds: "Il y a des plantes qui nous empoisonnet, des animaux qui nous dévorent, des talens qui nous sont pernicieux" (II, 538). If there is any salvation, it is to be found in rational and ethical interaction of the self and the world. "Die *Lehrjahre* sind die Dichtung der Wechselwirkung von Ich und Welt unter dem Gesichtspunkt der Ausbildung." (VII, 615) writes Trunz, and his comment applies to *La Nouvelle Héloïse*.

To achieve a rational form of self-limitation, it is necessary to have a sound knowledge of men. "Mon objet est de connoitre l'homme, et ma méthode de l'étudier dans ses diverses rélations" (II, 242). Once such understanding has been reached, Saint-Preux' true vocation (*Bestimmung*) becomes a reality unto himself: "Rien ne manque plus à mon bonheur, Milord m'a tout dit. Cher ami, je serai donc à vous? J'éleverai donc vos enfans? L'ainé des trois élevera les deux autres?" (II, 612). And is this desire to educate not matched by Wilhelm's awareness of his obligation to his son Felix?: "Er sah die Welt nicht mehr wie ein Zugvogel an . . . In diesem Sinne waren seine Lehrjahre geendigt, und mit dem Gefühl des Vaters hatte er auch alle Tugenden eines Bürgers erworben. Er fühlte es, und seiner Freude konnte nichts gleichen. 'O der unnötigen Strenge der Moral! rief er aus, 'da die Natur uns auf ihre liebliche Weise zu allem bildet, was wir sein sollen' " (VII, 502). Lothario completes this idea not without humor: ". . . was sogar die Frauen an uns ungebildet zurücklassen, das bilden die Kinder aus, wenn wir uns mit ihnen abgeben" (VII, 469).

La Nouvelle Héloïse is a *Bildungsroman*. But it is also a novel about lovers who try their best to overcome their feelings and to govern their conduct: "Si l'on n'est pas maitre de ses sentimens, au moins on l'est de sa conduite" (II, 644) states Claire, remembering *La Princesse de Clèves*. It is this primacy of the willful ethical act that led Kant to admire *La Nouvelle Héloïse,* and its center of gravity lay for him, according to Cassirer, "not in the romantic love story but in the second, 'moral' portion of the work."[23] The emergence of an *ethos freely conceived and determined* above and beyond passions relates the major theme of *La Nouvelle Héloïse* to one of the major assertions in *Wilhelm Meister:* "Des Menschen grösstes Verdienst bleibt wohl, wenn er die Umstände soviel als möglich bestimmt und sich so wenig als möglich von ihnen bestimmen lässt . . . Alles ausser uns ist nur Element, ja, ich darf wohl sagen, auch alles an uns; aber tief in uns liegt diese schöpferische Kraft, die das zu erschaffen vermag, was sein soll, und uns nicht ruhen und rasten lässt, bis wir es ausser uns oder an uns auf eine oder die andere Weise dargestellt haben" (VII, 405). *La Nouvelle Héloïse* illustrates dramatically this creative ethical force (*noumenal* in Kantian terms) which asserts itself in the love that Saint-Preux bears toward Julie who, unlike Dante's Beatrice, is transfigured without losing her humanity, that is to say, her mortality. "Non, quand je cesserai d'aimer la vertu, je ne t'aimerai plus . . . ," (II, 42) exclaims Saint-Preux at the outset of his calvary, and towards its end his friend Edouard consoles him by telling him that Julie *is* virtue: "Savez-vous ce qui vous a fait aimer toujours la vertu? Elle a pris à vos yeux la figure de cette femme adorable qui la réprésente si bien . . ." (II, 524). Indeed, he comes to love her more for the sake of his reason than his love for her: ". . . mais ce qui m'attache le plus à vous est le retour de ma raison. Elle vous montre à moi telle que vous êtes; elle vous sert mieux que l'amour même. Non, si j'étois resté coupable, vous ne me seriez pas aussi chere" (II, 674). And in his last letter to Julie which contains the famous *apostrophe:* "Femmes, femmes! objets chers et funestes . . ." (II, 676), Saint-Preux summarizes his dilemma in a manner that announces Goethe's "Zwei Seelen wohnen, ach, in meiner Brust": "Julie, en vérité, je crois avoir deux ames . . ." (II, 678). Natalie, too, is an example of virtue: "Unerreichbar wird immer die Handlungsweise bleiben, welche die Natur dieser schönen Selle vorgeschrieben hat" (VII, 608). Unlike Lotte (*Werther*), Charlotte (*Wahlverwandtschaften*), and Gretchen, Natalie remains a symbol of perfection. Julie, however, is real and because of her womanliness she expiates Rousseau's sense of guilt which, to my way of thinking, represents his primary existential experience . . . *sein Urerlebnis der Schuld.* Indeed, Julie's last words to Saint-Preux, beautiful and very moving, tell the sense of Saint-Preux' and Rousseau's tragedy: "La vertu qui nous sépara sur la terre, nous unira dans le séjour éternel. Je meurs dans cette douce attente. Trop heureuse d'acheter au prix de ma vie le droit de t'aimer toujours sans crime, et de te le dire encore une fois!" (II, 743).

Aimer sans crime! This wish expresses Rousseau's fondest dream. Related to the myth of the Golden Age, his anti-Augustinian and anti-Calvinistic vision of pure love "sans mistére et sans honte"

(I, 138) permeates all of Jean-Jacques' feeling and thinking and represents, as it were, the positive side of his guilt complex unquestionably initiated by his mother's death: "... Je coûtai la vie à ma mere ... (I, 7). *La Nouvelle Héloïse,* aside from its historical and auto-biographical implications (*l'Idylle des Cerises,* Mme de Warens, Claude Anet, Mme d'Houdetot and Lambert etc.), attempts to resolve the problem of how to love without committing a crime. The solution it offers is the concept of *vertu,* not *à la romaine,* but almost *à l'allemande,* and Cassirer has shown how Rousseau's meditations on the subject lead to Kant's categorical imperative. Virtue entails renunciation, and renunciation, in its purest form, turns to death. Julie, it has been noted, is *une grande sensuelle* and to forsake the senses is to forsake life. *Amour* is to Julie d'Etange what *plaisir* is to Manon Lescaut, and Des Grieux who turns his "inconstante Manon" into a good girl, kills her as surely as Saint-Preux, Julie. "Que de maux vous causez à ceux qui vous aiment!" (II, 307) complains Claire. *Bildung,* it would seem, also exacts its price from women. *Wilhelm Meisters Lehrjahre* corroborates this sad truth, for its hero causes Marianne's death, unwittingly, yet necessarily.

"Ich habe nun einmal gerade zu jener harmonischen Ausbildung meiner Natur, die mir meine Geburt versagt, eine unwiderstehliche Neigung" (VII, 291) writes Wilhelm to Werner. Can one speak of a similar desire for harmonious development in the case of Saint-Preux? Perhaps? Does this harmonious development occur in *Wilhelm Meisters Lehrjahre?* Kurt May thinks not, arguing that Goethe's novel diverges strongly from the ideal of the harmonious personality as described by Schiller in the sixth book of his *Briefe über die ästhetische Erziehung*—an ideal shaped by the thinking of Winckelmann, Herder, and Humboldt: "Zwischen dem neuhumanistischen Bildungsideal seiner Zeit und 'Wilhelm Meisters Lehrjahren' als Bildungsroman muss ein scharfer Trennungsstrich gezogen werden; d.h., zugleich zwischen dem idealistischen Menschenbild Schillers und den Neuhumanisten und ihrem Griechenbild einerseits, wie es im Brief über die ästhetische Erziehung vorgetragen wird, und andererseits dem Goetheschen Menschenbild der 'Lehrjahre', in dem sich sein mit Recht berühmter 'realistischer Tic' wunderbar bekundet hat."[24] And Kurt May concludes his perspicacious analysis as follows: "Zwei Jahre nach dem Erscheinen der 'Briefe über die ästhetische Erziehung' hat Goethe den deutsch-bürgerlichen Bildungsroman herausgebracht, der den Lebenssinn eines allseitig strebenden Menschen einschränkend zurückführt auf die schlichte Erkenntnis, dass sich ein deutschbürgerlicher Mensch zu einer bestimmten nützlichen Tätigkeit im Dienst der Gesellschaft zu entscheiden habe."[25] To be sure, esthetic considerations, specifically Shakespeare, occupy important moments in Wilhelm's development. Saint-Preux, less interested in art and art criticism, does, however, *en bon rousseauiste,* engage in a polemical attack against French tragedy, opera, and music. How then does it stand in regard to Saint-Preux' harmonious *Ausbildung?* Whereas Goethe's hero (not Goethe) tends to dissassociate the esthetic experience symbolized by his encounter with Shakespeare from his experience of a useful, virtuously active life, Saint-Preux (very much Rousseau) synthesizes esthetic and moral experience: "J'ai toujours cru," writes Saint-Preux to his *charmante écolière,* "que le bon n'étoit que le beau mis en action, que l'un tenoit intimement à l'autre, et qu'ils avoient tous deux une source commune dans la nature bien ordonnée. Il suit de cette idée que le goût se perfectionne par les mêmes moyens que la sagesse, et qu'une ame bien touchée des charmes de la vertu doit à proportion être aussi sensible à tous les autres genres de beautés" (II, 59). This important statement parallels a fundamental viewpoint of Rousseau, who steadfastly maintained the primacy of life over art throughout his social critique as well as in his autobiographical writings.

The second part of *La Nouvelle Héloïse* suggests analogies not only with *Wilhelm Meisters Lehrjahre,* but also with *Wilhelm Meisters Wanderjahre,* Goethe's *Altersroman.* The subtitle of *Die Wanderjahre* is *Die Entsagenden* (the renunciants). Renunciation permeates *La Nouvelle Héloïse* and much of its nobility emanates from the desperate attempt of its characters to metamorphose defeat into renunciation. Although the Wilhelm of the *Lehrjahre* avoids failure save for the death of Marianne and his departure from the theater, the last part of the novel announces gently the need of renunciation so deeply understood by the mature Goethe: "Lothario und seine Freunde können jede Art von Entsagung von mir fordern . . ." (VIII, 562). And a few pages further on: "Ängstlich ist es, immer zu suchen, aber viel ängstlicher, gefunden zu haben und verlassen zu müssen" (VII, 569). Saint-Preux and Julie are the true ancestors of all the renunciants of the great *Bildungs-*

romane, from Goethe's Wilhelm and his *schöne Seele* to Stifter's Gustav and Mathilde, from Keller's Heinrich und Judith to Thomas Mann's Hans Castorp.

"In der Tat kann man von diesem Roman sagen," wrote Schiller to Goethe, "Er ist nirgends beschränkt als durch die rein ästhetische Form, und wo die Form darin aufhört, da hängt er mit dem Unendlichen zusammen. Ich möchte ihn einer schönen Insel vergleichen, die zwischen zwei Meeren liegt" (VIII, 549). *La Nouvelle Héloïse* exhibits the same tendency toward isolation. Clarens, on the shores of Lake Geneva, far removed from large cities, becomes a shrine devoted to wholesome living which precludes too much contact. ". . . *on y sait vivre;*" exclaims Saint-Preux, "non dans le sens qu'on donne en France à ce mot, qui est d'avoir avec autrui certaines manieres établies par la mode; mais de la vie de l'homme, et pour laquelle il est né . . :" (II, 528, author's italics—the exclamation *on y sait vivre* turning into an admonition gracing the statue of the *Oheim* in Natalie's castle: "*Gedenke zu leben*" [VII, 540, also the author's italics]). Likewise, the plot of *Wilhelm Meister's Lehrjahre* unfolds, for the most part, far from the noise and agitation of towns. Clarens with its *salon d'Apollon* offers a refuge: ". . . c'est l'azile inviolable de la confiance, de l'amitié, de la liberté. C'est la société des cœurs qui lie en ce lieu celle de la table; elle est une sorte d'initiation à l'intimité, et jamais il ne s'y rassemble que des gens qui voudroient n'être plus séparés. Milord, la fête vous attend . . ." (II, 544). One should add parenthetically that the alpine scenes of *La Nouvelle Héloïse* resemble more those of the *Wanderjahre* than any one setting of the *Lehrjahre;* similarly the paternalistic world of Clarens ". . . où regnent l'ordre, la paix, l'innocence; où l'on voit réuni sans appareil, sans éclat, tout ce qui répond à la véritable destination de l'homme" (II, 441) calls to mind Goethe's description of the countryseat of the Oberamtmann in the chapter entitled "Wer ist der Verräter?"[26]

This structural isolation, also characteristic of parts of *Der grüne Heinrich, Der Nachsommer, Der Zauberberg* and Kafka's *Das Schloss* as well as of the more romantic *Bildungsromane,* like *Heinrich von Ofterdingen* and *Hyperion,* expresses an integral aspect of the psyche of the heroes of these novels. Like a self-developing Leibnitzian monad,[27] these youths realize within themselves their ethos and vocation, integrate in their lives the love of a woman and the advice of pedagogues, and seek to achieve a reconciliation between themselves and the world in which they must live. It is a key-idea of the late eighteenth century and early nineteenth century that man has to be his own redeemer, that he must bring about his salvation without recourse to transcendental agents. *Les Confessions* and *La Nouvelle Héloïse* sustain this viewpoint subtly and powerfully, and a few years after their completion, respectively in 1770 and 1761, Kant's *Kritik der reinen Vernunft*, 1781, proclaims the Copernican Revolution, namely, that the perceived world is man's creation in accordance with transcendental principles, a notion of incalculable importance, for it represents a theoretical point of departure for German Idealism and for Romantic art and criticism in general. The very possibility of realization of this revolutionary insight depended on Kant's refusal to make theoretical reason *constituitive* of *Being* as did Spinoza and Descartes. Reason without experience (*Erfahrung*) is impotent, experience without reason, blind. In 1799, shortly after the publication of *Wilhelm Meisters Lehrjahre* in 1796, Fichte announces the main tenets of his *Wissenschaftslehre*. Unlike Kant, who insists upon the phenomenological aspect of reality, as opposed to the noumenal reality manifesting itself only in the moral act, Fichte claims that the objective world *is* the work of the *produktive Einbildungskraft* or productive imagination. Reason, according to Fichte, does not know that the world it confronts is an unconscious projection by the Ego, and hence toils forever to overcome everything which stands in its way, discovering this or that to be its own, thus recovering incessantly the objectified and alienated parts of the self. Furthermore, asserts Fichte, this process of recovery has no end and becomes the vocation of man or *Die Bestimmung des Menschen*. The psychological implications of the Fichtean doctrine, derived from Kant and elaborated by Hegel, are already implicit in *La Nouvelle Héloïse* and *Les Confessions* and, at times, quite explicit in *Wilhelm Meisters Lehrjahre*. It would be folly to reduce this *Bildungsroman* to a Fichtean schema, not only because of the specific nature of Goethe's genius, but also because of his powerfully classical world view which does not favor self-deification or an excessive aggrandizement of the ego. Yet, *La Nouvelle Héloïse* and *Wilhelm Meisters Lehrjahre* do trace the measured progression of individuals, ever-obsessed by misunderstandings, haunted by questions, stimulated by errors, forever moving toward a higher degree of active self-realization and a serene awareness of the world. It is significant, moreover, that Friedrich Schlegel's famous pronouncement on *Wilhelm*

Meisters Lehrjahre relates Fichte and Goethe: "Die Französische Revolution, Fichtes *Wissenschaftslehre* und Goethes 'Meister' sind die grössten Tendenzen des Zeitalters." If one substitutes "Jean-Jacques Rousseau" for "French Revolution," Schlegel's views confirm our own (VIII, 554).

Whereas *La Nouvelle Héloïse* contains few humorous and witty incidents, *Wilhelm Meisters Lehrjahre* abounds with quips and cheerful scenes, especially at its beginning. "Das Merkwürdigste an dem Totaleindruck scheint mir dieses zu sein, dass Ernst und Schmerz durchaus wie ein Schattenspiel versinken und der leichte Humor vollkommen darüber Meister wird" (VIII, 529) comments Schiller. Its conclusion, however, like that of *La Nouvelle Héloïse,* tends to stress stately and conscious attitudes. "Schreitet, schreitet ins Leben zurück!" sing the youths at Mignon's funeral, "nehmet den heiligen Ernst mit hinaus, denn der Ernst, der heilige, macht allein das Leben zur Ewigkeit" (VII, 578). The style of both novels, especially in their middle parts and conclusions, reflects an essentially thoughtful mood; oratory and lyricism lose ground, and thought, pure thought, assumes an ever-increasing ascendancy over dramatic action and the spoken word. The language tends towards silence and meditation which find direct expression in *la matinée à l'anglaise*—this meditative mood being, however, enhanced for the purpose of contrast, by lyrical outbursts caused by the remembrance of things past, as for example, "la promenade sur le lac" or Wilhelm's discovery of Marianne's death.

Bildungsromane are, by the nature of things, sententious, and Rousseau and Goethe themselves, given to dispensing apodictic truths, make use of their narratives to regale their readers with numerous maxims. Samuel Johnson, Voltaire, Diderot and Wieland exhibit the same tendency; their maxims are, however, for the most part independent of the plot of the narrative in which they occur, be it *Rasselas, Candide, Le Neveu de Rameau* or *Agathon.* Neo-classical representatives of the Enlightenment, they shape and deliver their *traits* in the traditional manner of La Rochefoucauld and La Bruyère. Rousseau and Goethe, while influenced by the classical tradition of the *sententiae,* modify maxims by integrating them into the plots of their respective narratives and their personal lives so that their sayings have a greater warmth than those of their predecessors. The classical maxim has become a *Lebensweisheit,* tinged with a touch of personal tragedy and wit—a desire and need of intimacy, developed *à outrance* by Baudelaire and

Nietzsche. Goethe was conscious of this modification of the role and sense of the traditional maxim: " 'Ich habe immer gesehen,'" versetzte Natalie, 'dass unsere Grundsätze nur ein Supplement zu unsern Existenzen sind' " (VII, 565). Generally, the mood of Rousseau's and Goethe's maxims is similar. Indeed, certain of the former's aphorisms are purely Goethean in concept and form: "L'humanité coule comme une eau pure et salutaire, et va fertiliser les lieux bas; elle cherche toujours le niveau . . ." (II, 304) or "La nature . . . veut que les enfans soient enfans avant que d'être hommes" (II, 562) or elsewhere "Non, mon enfant, l'ame n'a point de sexe . . ." (II, 629). Witty aphorisms such as "Die Vaterschaft beruht überhaupt nur auf der Überzeugung; ich bin überzeugt, und also bin ich Vater" (VII, 559) do not have their counterpart in Rousseau who was too vulnerable to make quips about fatherhood, although some of Saint-Preux' remarks are, it must be confessed, unwittingly funny: "Je l'aime trop pour l'épouser"[28] (II, 679).

Even a cursory review of European literature reveals the surprising rarity of the major themes of the *Bildungsroman* as defined by *La Nouvelle Héloïse* and *Wilhelm Meisters Lehrjahre*. The characteristics of these novels are the presence of a young man in whom grows a vocation, an ethos, a sense of commitment towards the society in which he lives. The youth is advised, guided by mentors and sages, initiated into various societies, as well as formed by the love of women, who will often be sacrificed or who sacrifice themselves in a real or symbolic manner. Perhaps the most important aspect of the *Bildungsroman* is the insistence on a self-generating ethos, in other words, moral values must not be given to the youth in the form of dogma, injunction, rite etc., but must be arrived at by trial and error, by a process of inner purification of which the youth, while engaged in it, need not necessarily be conscious. A major reason for the relative and surprising scarcity of the theme of the self-generating ethos lies in the antecedents of Western literature. Thus, the idea of *Becoming* or *Werden* appears alien to mythology which according to Kerényi "is never the biography of the gods as often appears to the observer." "It is always," he continues, "less than a biography, even though it tells of the birth and the childhood of the gods, the deeds of their youth, and sometimes of their early death. The remarkable thing about these childish or youthful feats is that they show the god in the full perfection of his power and outward form, and thus really preclude biographical thinking—thinking in periods of life as stages of development."[29] Classical literature parallels the refusal of mythology to portray growth, the celebrated exception to the rule being the *Telemacheia* section of Homer's *Odyssey*. Disputing the claim that the story of Telemachus implies the maturation of a character, Wilamowitz asserts categorically: "Charakterentwicklung zu verfolgen liegt der hellenischen Poesie, liegt überhaupt den Hellenen fern. Es ist auch in den späteren Büchern von einer Veränderung im Wesen Telemachs nichts zu spüren. Die Sache liegt wohl anders."[30] Werner Jaeger summarizes an opposing view: "The antitype of the relentless Achilles is the mild Telemachus. In the first book of the *Odyssey* we are shown something of his education. While Achilles rejects the teachings of Phoenix and meets his doom thereby, Telemachus gives willing ear to the counsels of the goddess Athena, disguised as his father's friend Mentes. But the advice of Mentes is the same as the promptings of Telemachus' own heart. He is in fact the pattern of the docile youth who is led on to glory by accepting the advice of an experienced friend. In the succeeding books Athena . . . disguises herself as another old friend, Mentor, and accompanies Telemachus to Pylus and Sparta . . . Mentor watches every step his pupil takes and helps him at every turn, with kindly words and wise advice."[31] In a subtle article, Howard Clarke measures *le pour et le contre* and concludes that "Telemachus' journey is neither unnecessary nor unmotivated, although the necessity is Telemachus himself and the motive transcends the averred search for information."[32] But aside from the *Telemacheia* and Sophocles' *Philoctetes*, where the son of Achilles, Neoptolemos, is seen wavering, developing, maturing, Greek literature presents us with characters devoid of "internal development" in the Rousseauean and Goethean sense of the word, for, it must be remembered, it was the task of philosophy and to a lesser extent of religion to concern itself with ethico-maturational processes. To be sure, Oedipus and Pentheus develop insight into the nature of their selves, their destiny and their concomitant tragedy; the absolute, however, is given to them and to the degree that they struggle against it, they become, according to Hegel, tragic in essence. In his *Mimesis*, Erich Auerbach confirms the prevailing views on the relatively static nature of the classical conception of the human character: "In the mimetic literary art of antiquity, the instability of fortune almost always appears as a fate which strikes from without and affects only a limited area, not as a fate which results from the inner processes of the real, historical world[33] . . . the ancients' ways of viewing things . . . does not see forces, it sees vices and virtues, successes and mistakes."[34] Auerbach concludes his exposition on the technique of character delineation of Petronius and Tacitus: "At times we even find traces of an ontogenetic derivation of individual characters, as for example in Sallust's portrait of Catiline and especially in Tacitus' portrait of Tiberius. But this is the limit which cannot be passed. The ethical and rhetorical approach are incompatible with a conception in which reality is a development of forces."[35]

Despite the fact that the Judeo-Christian tradition is other-worldly and dogmatic (the Law is given), the *Confessions* of St. Augustine offer the first example of a true autobiography, namely the story of a child that grows from within into manhood, finds its vocation through trial and error, and discovers salvation through the grace of God. To the extent that St. Augustine analyzes and evokes with unparalleled brilliance the formative development of his senses, emotions, passions, his soul, and destiny, the *Confessions* represent the first literary paradigm of the *Bildungsroman* with-out, however, exhibiting the factor of the self-generating ethos.

True to the classical model, the epic tradition does not concern itself with questions concerning inner growth. Beowulf, Roland, the Cid, remain what they are when we first meet them. Kriem-hilde, to be sure, changes into a *valandinne;* rather than generat-ing an ethos, her character, bent on vengeance, degenerates, that is, loses strength. Unlike epic heroes, the knights of the Arthurian Romances have personalities that seem to evolve by subtle degrees —their inner growth proceeding in stages carefully matched by initiatory rites and allegorical events which exemplify the ideals of the late twelfth century. Their Middle High German counter-parts reflect this new concern with spiritual maturation, especially Parzival, whom Melitta Gerhard considers to be the first hero of the German *Entwicklungsroman*, a point of departure of a trend, which by way of *Simplizissimus* and *Agathon* culminates accord-ing to her in *Wilhelm Meisters Lehrjahre*. Neither the allegorical tradition of Jean de Meung's *Roman de la Rose,* nor Dante's poetic and spiritual quest of *La Vita Nuova* offers analogues or resemblances to what will be the *Bildungsroman*. The great story tellers, Boccaccio and Chaucer relate what happens to various characters rather than illuminating the processes that might ac-count for their behavior. With the advent of the Renaissance, the themes of education, autobiography, and organic development are stressed by Castiglione, Rabelais and Montaigne, but not within the context of a fictional narrative. Owing to its autobiographical orientation, the picaresque novel approaches to some extent the concept of the *Bildungsroman* without, however, integrating in its plot the idea of a spiritual and ethical growth. Thus, *Lazarillo de Tormes*, stresses, above all, epistemological developments in the mind of its young hero whose initiation into life at the hand of the blind man and the miserly priest lead to an *éducation brutale* which disregards the realization of his potential. Like a godless Adam, comments Claudio Guillén, Lazarillo rediscovers all values anew and "unable to either join or in fact reject his fellowmen, he chooses to compromise and live the life of a 'half-outsider.' "³⁶ The narrative voice, ironic, detached, avoids all semblance of renunciation. Whether or not is is possible to interpret *Don Quixote* in terms of *Bildung* remains open to doubt, since, however youthful and poetic in attitudes, the Knight of the Sad Countenance hardly fits the model of a youth awakening to life.

Drama, by its very nature, little suited to depicting the phenomenon of gradual growth by trial and error, prefers to project on the stage identities in a state of crisis, tense, ready to burst forth as do Sigismondo, Macbeth and Phèdre. "Racinian heroes" comments Odette de Mourgues "stand, so to speak, from the beginning of eternity, with all the potential catastrophic violence of their passions ready to explode. The provocation must come from the outside and take the form of an external event."³⁷ By way of exception, we have already referred to Sophocles' Neoptolemus as a character in a state of flux; one should also add Seneca's Medea whose *Medea fiam* suggests a somber sense of *Werden* that culminates in her final cry *Medea nunc sum*.³⁸ Mention should be made of Shakespeare's Prince Hal who, in the course of *Henry IV Part 1*, *Henry IV Part II*, and *Henry V*, develops from a seeming wastrel into an ideal king. Corneille's *Cinna* also presents a young hero trying to become a man. His maturation coincides with the plot, and offers an example of a delicate balance of the Aristotelian concepts of character and plot; indeed, of all neo-classical plays, *Cinna* seems to me most prophetic of the ideals of the Enlightenment by virtue of its insistence that one's ethos results from an organic fusion of error and maturation, will and destiny.³⁹ Furthermore, Milton's epic-dramatic evocation of Adam exhibits elements tending towards the *Bildungsroman*.

It is in no way surprising that Rousseau should have availed himself of the genre of the novel to define his ideas concerning self-generating virtue. With his natural love of the *genre:* "Ma mere avoit laissé des Romans." (I, 8) and his autodidactic and Protestant background, Rousseau possessed the prerequisites to engage in a *libre examen de conscience.* Moreover, his autobiographical and pedagogical genius, his need and power to develop for himself and his world a new ethos as well as his native yearning for *Innerlichkeit,* combined with the general *Umwertung der Werte* of the Age of Enlightenment to make possible the conception and the creation of *La Nouvelle Héloïse.* It should be stressed that this intense process of fictional interiorization occurred almost simultaneously with the appearance of *Candide* and *Rasselas* which stress exteriorization, satire, adventure, and characters compounded out of logic and hypotheses.

Given the extraordinary situation of Rousseau in regard to French culture and literature, *La Nouvelle Héloïse* occupies an equally extraordinary role in the history of French letters.[40] Disregarding for the sake of discussion conceptual complications concerning the sense of literary history in general, one finds it difficult to integrate Jean-Jacques' novel into a traditional frame of reference concerning French narrative fiction consisting of values as traditional as Chrétien's irony, Madame de La Fayette's lucidity and Balzac's visionary powers of evocation and so forth. And as it is awkward to fit *La Nouvelle Héloïse* into that illusory and yet ever so real French scheme of things, so it is relatively easy to relate Rousseau's novel in terms of its stated and unstated aspirations to *Wilhelm Meisters Lehrjahre, Der Nachsommer,* the second part of *Der grüne Heinrich* and *Der Zauberberg.* Try as one may, one cannot qualify either *Le rouge et le noir,* or *La Chartreuse de Parme* as a *Bildungsroman,* not so much because either lacks structural and thematic analogues (on the contrary, these abound), but because Julien and Fabrice yearn for love and not for *Bildung* in the Rousseauean and Goethean sense of the term. It is pertinent that Julien, attempting to conquer Amanda Binet, endowed with "une imagination de dame de comptoir, "dazzles her with quotations from *La Nouvelle Héloïse* as she sits behind her desk in a café in Besançon, and one may safely assume that the quotations were drawn from the first part—the message of the last part, admired by Kant and Mendelssohn, always having been lost on the French until, having undergone Hegelian and Heideggerian metamorphoses, it reappeared in France under the guise of Sartre's moral philosophy. Stendhal and Balzac are historical realists in Lukács' sense of the word, and in 1830, the Rousseauean and Goethean paternalistic and utopian world views with their concomitant emphasis on personal salvation through integration and renunciation, had long since given way to philosophies stressing individuation and struggle within, and against, an urban and industrial world. Thus, Balzac's *Illusions perdues*[41] by its very title announces the loss of a given faith. Lucien de Rubempré cannot be said to be capable of generating his own ethos and vocation; similarly, Frédéric Moreau incarnates Flaubert's attempt to trace "l'histoire morale des hommes de [sa] génération"[42]—a history characterized by feelings of loss and impotence. Sainte-Beuve's quip "mûrir, mûrir, on ne mûrit point, on pourrit" summarizes admirably the state of mind of the second part of the nineteenth century, and one has to wait for the emergence of Proust's *A la recherche du temps perdu* to encounter in France some of the major themes of the *Bildungsroman*, transmuted, to be sure, by the *engagement esthétique* as defined by Flaubert, who transformed the notion of salvation by way of dedication to art. Proust's novel is, in part, the story of a vocation and *Bildung* in the Goethean sense, and the relationship between Rousseau and Proust remains to be studied.

Shifting attention to the English tradition,[43] one finds that Richardson's novels, although crucial to the development of the genre of the novel, do not contain the *sine qua non* of the *Bildungsroman*, the self-generated ethos within a youthful growing personality, since he pits virtue and helplessness against authority and injustice as in *Pamela*, or against lust and viciousness as in *Clarissa Harlowe*. As for the sense of *Tom Jones* which has been mentioned as an antecedent to *Wilhelm Meister*, one need only to recall Fielding's own assertion that he described *manners* not men. *Great Expectations*, however, could lend itself to thematic comparisons with the Rousseauean and Goethean models because Pips' quest for identity proceeds gradually by way of trial and error; moreover, he is guided from afar by Abel Magwitch, alias Provis,—the mentor being an ex-criminal, but still a guide. Although the indexes of major studies of the English novel of the nineteenth and twentieth centuries do not even list the word *Bildungsroman*, the fact of the matter is that Joseph Conrad's *Lord Jim* conforms surprisingly to the literary concept under discussion. Its hero, held under the spell of "Imagination, the enemy of men,"[44] impedes the progress of truth within him. Moral discovery seems to be the object of Conrad's tales, and *Lord Jim* embodies this need to come to terms with one's destiny. Being a novel of the turn of the century, *Lord Jim* establishes an equilibrium between the belief in the possibility of character and ethos, courage and destiny on the one hand, and on the other, a disbelief in the chance of personal salvation. Given this kind of interpretation, *The Heart of Darkness* becomes the *Bildungsroman à revers,* as it were. Furthermore, the structure of *Lord Jim* exhibits other elements of the *Bildungsroman;* the action, occurring in an insular setting, presents all the characteristics of what Schiller calls "die schöne Zweckmässigkeit," (VIII, 540) that is to say, a beautiful purposefulness, which the hero lives without being aware of it: ". . . der Held hat keinen Plan, aber das Stück ist planvoll" (VII, 254). A woman is sacrificed (Jewel), the action is to some extent guided by a latter-day *Turmgesellschaft,* Marlow and Stein, alias l'Abbé and Lothario, alias M. de Wolmar, alias Fénelon's Mentor, alias Pallas Athena, protectress of Telemachos. Conrad's novel offers a remarkable innovation of the Goethean pattern in that it creates dramatic tension between the controllers themselves, that is, Stein and Marlow, chief members of a metaphysical high court pondering the fate of their charge. The chief-justices too are on trial: "Was it for my own sake that I wish to find some shadow of an excuse for that young fellow, whom I had never seen before . . . ,"[45] asks Marlow of himself. Indeed, Conrad scholars would do well in making *Wilhelm Meisters Lehrjahre* their *vade mecum!*

It would be equally fruitful, I believe, to contrast the structure of the other masterpiece of the end of the nineteenth century, Henry James' *The Wings of the Dove* with *La Nouvelle Héloïse* and *Wilhelm Meister.* Merton Densher is young, malleable if not weak, led, cajoled and guided respectively by Kate Croy, Aunt Maud, and Sir Luke, and eventually "saved" by Millie Theale who plays the role of the sacrificial woman and redeemer. But whereas Saint-Preux, Wilhelm Meister and perhaps Jim achieve some sort of salvation by virtue of an autonomous power within their psyches, Merton Densher, it would seem, changes for having been grazed by the wings of the dove. "We shall never be again as we were"—this last judgment by Kate points to the intervention of a miraculous power and because of the suggestion of the Christian

mystery reminiscent of Dostoyevsky's *Idiot,* it would appear difficult to interpret Merton Densher as a young man capable of shaping his own values and destiny.

For historical and political reasons, neither Russian, Italian nor
Spanish nineteenth century literature offers fictional narratives
that approach in design and intent our Rousseauean and Goethean
models of the *Bildungsroman.* For only civilizations that experienced totally the cultural experience of the Enlightenment in its
broadest sense, that is to say, France, Germany, and England, could
keep alive until the twentieth century the vision, dream or concept, nay memory of, an individual capable of redeeming himself
—of a young man, who, by living and elaborating his vocation
and destiny, comes to terms with the world in which he must live.
Whether Kafka's K., Joyce's Dedalus, Proust's narrator, and Beckett's cripple are descendents of Saint-Preux and Wilhelm Meister
must remain doubtful.[46] And it remains even more doubtful, I
fear, whether there will ever occur again a suspension of the col-
lision of universal forces, a moment of luminous freedom, when
men will think themselves capable of saving their own souls.

CHAPTER IV

Jean-Jacques Rousseau's *Confessions*
and
Gottfried Keller's *Der Grüne Heinrich*

Et ecce infantia mea olim mortua
est et ego vivo. (St. Augustine, *Confessions*)

In einem biographischen Versuch
ziemt es wohl von sich selbst zu reden.
(Goethe, *Dichtung und Wahrheit*)

Rousseau's name appears rarely in criticism devoted to Gottfried Keller's *Der grüne Heinrich*.[1] The reasons for this neglect are complex, the most obvious being Keller's reticence to pronounce himself clearly concerning the author of the *Confessions* which, I am convinced, represent a source of inspiration for the first and the second version of *Der grüne Heinrich,* specifically, for the so-called *Jugendgeschichte.* To be sure, Keller mentions Rousseau's name, but seemingly at random and in a manner that is detached, ironical, and sometimes pejorative, as for instance, in a letter to Emil Palleske, dated Berlin, Dec. 4, 1835: "Scherenberg habe ich, nach langer Unterbrechung, erst in letzter Zeit, als er von ziemlich schwerer Krankeit genas, einigemal besucht. Da er aber, obgleich er sich kaum rühren konnte, sich gleich wieder in seiner ausgehöhlten unwahren Manier lustig erging und mit koketten Rousseau-spielen und erlogenem Wohlwollen um sich warf, wurde ich wieder für eine Zeitlang abgeschreckt."[2] In a letter to Friedrich Theodor Vischer, dated August 6, 1877, he writes concerning Emil Kuh's biography of Hebbel: "... ich glaube nicht, dass *in puncto* Menschlichkeiten einer das Recht hat, die Rousseausche Offenheit und Geschwätzigkeit im Namen eines andern so weit zu treiben ..."[3] The allusion, however, which has decisively determined critical thought occurs in his third autobiographical essay of 1876.

Mein Malkasten war längst zugeschlossen und jenes unheizbare Atelier verlassen, und so zog ich zum zweiten Male aus, um an deutschen Schulen, wo es gut schien, meinen Aufenthalt zu nehmen.

Auf diesen Fahrten nahm ich den einst angefangenen Roman wieder zur Hand, dessen Titel "Der grüne Heinrich" schon existierte. Ich gedachte immer noch, nur einen mässigen Band zu schreiben; wie ich aber etwas vorrückte, fiel mir ein, die Jugendgeschichte des Helden oder vielmehr Nichthelden als Autobiographie einzuschalten mit Anlehnung an Selbsterfahrenes und —empfundenes. Ich kam darüber in ein solches Fabulieren hinein, dass das Buch vier Bände stark und ganz unförmlich wurde. Ursache hiervon war, dass ich eine unbezwingliche Lust daran fand, in der vorgerückten Tageszeit einen Lebensmorgen zu erfinden, den ich nicht gelebt hatte, oder, richtiger gesagt, die dürftigen Keime und Ansätze zu meinem Vergnügen poetisch auswachsen zu lassen. Jedoch ist die eigentlich Kindheit sogar das Anekdotische darin, so gut wie wahr, hier und da bloss, in einem letzten Anfluge von Nachahmungstrieb, von der konfessionellen Herbigkeit Rousseaus angehaucht, obgleich nicht allzu stark . . .

Dagegen ist die reifere Jugend des grünen Heinrich zum grössten Teile ein Spiel der ergänzenden Phantasie und sind namentlich die beiden Frauengestalten gedichtete Bilder der Gegensätze, wie sie im erwachenden Leben des Menschen sich bestreiten (XXI, 20, 1).

The phrase which has led the majority of German and Swiss critics astray is of course "Jedoch ist die eigentliche Kindheit . . . hier und da bloss . . . von der konfessionellen Herbigkeit Rousseaus angehaucht, obgleich nicht allzu stark." Somewhat ambiguous, the statement suggests a limited influence at most. Whatever the precise meaning of the *konfessionelle Herbigkeit* may be, Baechtold, Ermatinger, and others have interpreted Keller's remarks as a fair estimation of his debt to Rousseau. Such too, is the view of Therese Seiler whose dissertation *Gottfried Keller und die französische Literatur,* Zürich 1955, limits itself to an incomplete recapitulation of orthodox opinions concerning the relationship between Rousseau and Keller. Although she admits to a "seltsame geistige Verwandtschaft" between the two compatriots, her conclusion denies the possibility of any proof of influence: "Wenn jedoch die Interpretation, obgleich sie ähnliche Motive in den beiden Werken [*Les Confessions* and *Der grüne Heinrich*] aufzeigen kann, den Nachweis der Beeinflussung durch Rousseau zu liefern ausserstande ist, so liegt der Grund im Thema selber."[4] It is fortunate that Keller has had more perspicacious readers, for instance, Varnhagen von Ense, *der Statthalter Goethes auf Erden,* who wrote in his journal in 1854 on the date of the publication of the first three volumes of Keller's novel: "Sein 'Grüner Heinrich' ist ein Roman, wie Rousseaus *Bekenntnisse einer* ist, voll Psychologie, unbeabsichtigter Pädagogik, frischer Naturbilder, alles in edler, höherer Haltung . . ."[5] The first scholars to investigate the relationship under discussion were M. Cornicelius[6] and W. H. Faulkner,[7] the former writing a penetrating essay in 1905 which has been ignored, the latter suggesting in 1912 a parallelism between Rousseau's childhood loves, Mlle Goton and Mlle de Vulson, and Keller's Judith and Anna—a viewpoint later confirmed by Ermatinger.

The only critic to have ever attempted a socio-political confrontation of Rousseau and Keller is Georg Lukács. After calling Keller the greatest German realist and the greatest *Erzähler* since Goethe and E. T. A. Hoffman, he compares the Citizen of Geneva with the *Staatsschreiber* of Zürich, opposing the former's revolutionary and universal commitment to social change (at least on the theoretical level) to the latter's supposedly inefficient contribution to Swiss democracy.[8] Making some allowance for ideological bias, Lukács' remarks may be interpreted as characteristic of critics who have evaluated *Der grüne Heinrich* according to the genre of the *Bildungsroman*[9] or *Erziehungsroman* patterned on *Wilhelm Meister*. The most prominent and sensible of these, Ermatinger, after reviewing Keller's intermittently reverential attitude toward Goethe, declares: "Man denkt, wenn man von einem Parallelismus zwischen Keller und Goethe spricht, wohl an erster Stelle an den *Wilhelm Meister* und den *Grünen Heinrich*. Goethe lässt in den *Lehrjahren* seinen Wilhelm Meister herauswachsen aus der Ichbezogenheit des Bildungsästheten des 18. Jahrhunderts in die gemeinnützige Gesellschaftsbildung des 19. Schönheit und Nutzen stehen sich gegenüber, und die eine muss dem andern weichen. Die *Wanderjahre* führen diese Entwicklung weiter."[10] Ermatinger goes on to draw analogies between Wilhelm's and Heinrich's *Kunstträume* and their respective willingness to renounce these ambitions in favor of a socially and politically productive life, concluding: "Im *Wilhelm Meister*, auch in den *Wanderjahren*, ist die Wandlung der Zeit von der ästhetischen zur praktischen Lebensauffassung von der fernen Geistigkeit des achtzehnten Jahrhunderts aus gesehen. Im *Grünen Heinrich* ist sie tatsächlich dargestellt. Das erklärt, warum im *Grünen Heinrich* alles Leben so viel sinnlicher und anschaulicher gestaltet ist als im *Wilhelm Meister*. Gegenüber dem nur bedingt deutschen Charakter des Stoffes im

Wilhelm Meister ist der Wirklichkeitsgehalt des *Grünen Heinrich* durchaus schweizerisch."[11]

Other critics, among them Agnes Waldhausen,[12] have judged Keller's novel on the basis of norms and ideals derived from *Dichtung und Wahrheit*, taking as their point of departure the well-known passage in which Heinrich Lee tells of his passionate encounter with Goethe: "So hatte ich noch einmal diesen Himmel durchschweift und vieles wieder doppelt gelesen und entdeckte zuletzt noch einen ganz neuen hellen Stern: *Dichtung und Wahrheit*" (V, 4). It is worthwhile to mention *en passant* that Keller's reaction to Goethe's autobiography is not unlike Goethe's reaction to Rousseau's *Confessions:* "Nur ein paar Blätter, die ich drinnen [*Les Confessions*] gesehen habe, sind wie leuchtende Sterne . . ." (In a letter to Charlotte von Stein, May 9, 1782).[13] And when the antiquarian removes the forty volumes of Goethe's complete works, Heinrich feels "als ob eine Schar glänzender und singender Geister die Stube verliessen" (V, 5).

Indeed, either viewpoint, that is, relating *Der grüne Heinrich* to *Wilhelm Meister* or to *Dichtung und Wahrheit*, results in meaningful comparisons only as long as one stresses the characteristically Goethean features of Keller's autobiographical novel, especially strong in its second part. However, all of these comparisons and ensuing generalizations break down or become inappropriate as soon as one attempts to account for the antecedent of the *Jugendgeschichte*. The *nature* of its autobiographical approach, its ego-oriented themes, and its *lyrico-realistic* mood do not conform to the Goethean prototypes. I have italicized the three terms because if one were to disregard their implications, Agnes Waldhausen's thesis that *Dichtung und Wahrheit* represents in perfection what he, Keller, tried to accomplish would be more acceptable. But, as matters stand, what Keller achieved in his *Jugendgeschichte* differs profoundly in quality and kind from anything any other German author ever wrote. This discrepancy, this originality would be relatively unimportant were it not for the fact that ever since its publication, discerning readers have insisted unequivocally on their preference for the *Jugendgeschichte*, declaring it to be the best part of *Der grüne Heinrich*. For instance, Hettner, in a letter to Keller, dated February 19, 1854: "Ich sage Ihnen die Wahrheit, diese Jugendgeschichte ist ein Juwel . . . und der Roman ungleich schwächer als jene."[14] Hofmannsthal's judgment is more extreme: "Wie schön wäre das Buch, wenn es nur seinen Anfang hätte und das andere verlorengegangen wäre."[15] Thus, depending on one's taste and literary orientation as well as on the focus of one's attention, Keller's autobiographical novel assumes a surprisingly large number of divergent historico-literary antecedents. Frieda Jaeggi,[16] for example, traces in the *Jugendgeschichte* the influence of Keller's infatuation for Jean Paul and the sense of his later rejection of him, while Walter Muschg considers Jeremias Gotthelf as the one great inspiration in the conception of such chapters as "Die Sippschaft."[17] Majut, however, chooses to highlight historical antecedents of the novel's psychological components: ". . . 'Der grüne Heinrich' ist kein Entwicklungsroman im eigentlichen Sinne der Sondergattung. Seinem inneren Romantypus nach liegt 'Der grüne Heinrich' vielmehr auf der Linie von Moritz' 'Anton Reiser' und Rousseaus 'Confessions.' "[18]

Less dogmatic and more inclusive is the viewpoint of Barker Fairley, who affirms: "The net result was a novel in which the finest traditions of German fiction were embodied. *Der grüne Heinrich* has the poetry and inwardness of the Romantic school, the psychological acumen of Moritz, the raciness of Seume, the folk-qualities of Jung-Stilling, the intellectual courage and something at least of the constructive thought of Goethe, combined with an unerring gift of objective visualization."[19] And after discussing possible influences by Richter and Mörike, he adds: "Of foreign writers Rousseau alone can be directly traced in the text and the spirit of *Der grüne Heinrich*."[20] He goes on to juxtapose Heinrich's youthful attempts at necromancy with "Rousseau's disaster in the *Confessions*, Pt. I, Bk. V"[21] (the real disaster in this book is Jean-Jacques' initiation to love by *Maman* rather than his "un-Panglossian" efforts in experimental physics) as well as Rousseau's characterization of Mme de Warens with Keller's reflections in the third chapter of *Der grüne Heinrich*. The reference that Fairley associates with the theological implications of the Pumpernickel episode reads: "Quand il n'y auroit eu de morale chrétienne je crois qu'elle l'auroit suivie, tant elle s'adaptoit bien à son caractère" (p. 230). In fact, this passage, supposedly a source of inspiration for Keller, relates how M. de Tavel's doctrine would have allowed Maman to sleep every day with twenty men "en repos de conscience" (p. 230). And Fairley concludes with unwitting irony: "It is perhaps not unfitting to leave *Der grüne Heinrich* thus associated. Whilst its Goethean qualities have been long recognized, its mental attitude places it more truly somewhere between Goethe and Rousseau."[22]

With this last sentence I agree wholeheartedly, since it is my conviction that the relationship between Rousseau's and Goethe's views on autobiography must be clarified first before there can be a meaningful understanding of the literary antecedents of Keller's autobiographical achievements in *Der grüne Heinrich* in general, and specifically, in the *Jugendgeschichte*. Fortunately, there exists a brilliant essay on the subject-matter by Martin Sommerfeld, who writes:

Rousseaus *Bekenntnisse* sind ein Ergebnis konsequenter Selbstanalyse, ja sie suchen hierin ihren Wert. Aber niemals hat Goethe, auch nicht in den selbstquälerischen, ja selbstzerstörerischen Epochen seiner Jugend, das Bedürfnis gehabt oder es über sich gebracht, seinem Ich wie einem Spiegel gegenüberzutreten und sich selbst zu analysieren. Wie sein Wilhelm Meister hält er das für ideale Biographie, wo man 'sein Bild ausser sich, zwar nicht wie im Spiegel sein zweites Selbst, sondern wie im Portrait als ein anderes Selbst' erblickt. Goethe hat sich selbst gelegentlich porträtiert (und *Dichtung und Wahrheit* ist das grosszügigste und treueste Porträt), nie aber analysiert . . . und was Goethes Autobiographie betrifft, so ist es das furchtbarste, nein: das einzig mögliche Missverständnis, *Dichtung und Wahrheit* für eine Synthese, gewonnen aus selbstanalytischen Erkenntnissen zu halten . . . Mit einem Wort: Goethes Selbstaussagen, auch diejenigen seiner Jugendzeit, wollen allenfalls die in seiner Natur wirksamen Kräfte, ihr Verhältnis zueinander, aussprechen, niemals aber die Bedingungen seines Seins analytisch ergründen . . . Genau dies aber will Rousseau, und eben hiermit ist er in der Geschichte der europäischen Seele Führer und Verführer geworden.[23]

Contrary to St. Augustine and Rousseau, Goethe does not want to explore the self in the Augustinian palaces of memory "ubi sunt thesauri innumerabilium imaginum,"[24] but seeks to determine the truth in the relationship between the individual and the world: "Nehmen wir sodann das bedeutende Wort vor: *Erkenne dich selbst*, so müssen wir es nicht im asketischen Sinne auslegen. Es ist keineswegs die Heautognosie unserer modernen Hypochondristen, Humoristen und Heautontimorumenen damit gemeint; sondern es heisst ganz einfach: Gib einigermassen Acht auf dich selbst, nimm Notiz von dir selbst, damit du gewahr werdest, wie du zu deinesgleichen und der Welt zu stehen kommst."[25] Goethe's autobiographical effort is all-embracing. In the words of R. Pascal: ". . . he tells of his imagination and feeling, of how and why experiences turned into poetry, but also gives a history of his times, a history of literature and thought, the development of his own

life and thought, and is ultimately concerned with a general problem arising from his total experience, the relation between freedom and necessity, between the infinitude of what is given him
and the particularity of what he makes of it, between conscious
intention and the 'daemon' within him."[26]

Rousseau, on the other hand, turns upon himself: "Je voudrois
pouvoir en quelque façon rendre mon ame transparente aux yeux
du lecteur, et pour cela je cherche à la lui montrer sous tous les
points de vue, à l'éclairer par tous les jours, à faire en sorte qu'il
ne s'y passe pas un mouvement qu'il n'apperçoive, afin qu'il puisse
juger par lui-même du principe qui les produit" (p. 175). Guided
by "la chaîne des sentimens" (p. 278) he cannot be mistaken.
Everything must be unveiled before his reader: ". . . il faut que je
me tienne incessamment sous ses yeux, qu'il me suive dans tous
les égaremens de mon cœur, dans tous les recoins de ma vie; qu'il
ne me perde pas de vue un seul instant, de peur que, trouvant
dans mon récit la moindre lacune, le moindre vide, et se demandant, qu'a-t-il fait durant ce tems-là, il ne m'accuse de n'avoir
pas voulu tout dire" (pp. 59, 60).

Such are some of the contrasts and oppositions between the
Rousseauean and Goethean philosophies on the sense and limits
of autobiography, and with these fragments in mind, Keller's
statements on autobiography and self-knowledge become almost
self-explanatory in regard to their intellectual and literary antecedents. But, unlike Rousseau and Goethe, Keller was no theorist.
His opinions are scattered and often embodied in his journals,
correspondence, and narratives, as for instance, in the *Sinngedicht*
in which he enumerates what may have been his *sources livresques:*
"Von den Blättern des heiligen Augustinus bis zu Rousseau und
Goethe fehlte keine der wesentlichen Bekenntnisfibeln, und neben
dem wilden und prahlerischen Benvenuto Cellini duckte sich das
fromme Jugendbüchlein Jung Stillings. Arm in Arm rauschten und
knisterten die Frau von Sévigné und der jüngere Plinius einher,
hintendrein wanderten die armen Schweizerbursche Thomas
Platter und Ulrich Bräcker, der arme Mann im Toggenburg"
(XI, 35, 6).

Why this concern with autobiography? The answer is simple,
replies Lucie, the heroine of the story:

Ich suche die Sprache der Menschen zu verstehen, wenn sie von sich
selbst reden; aber es kommt mir zuweilen vor, wie wenn ich durch einen
Wald ginge und das Gezwitscher der Vögel hörte, ohne ihrer Sprache

kundig zu sein. Manchmal scheint mir, dass Jeder etwas anderes sagt als
er denkt, oder wenigstens nicht recht sagen kann, was er denkt, und
dass dieses sein Schicksal sei. . . . Der bekennt alle sieben Todessünden und
verheimlicht, dass er an der linken Hand nur vier Finger hat . . . Wenn
ich sie nun alle so miteinander vergleiche in ihrer Aufrichtigkeit, die sie
für kristallklar halten, so frage ich mich: gibt es überhaupt ein mensch-
liches Leben, an welchem nichts zu verhehlen ist, das heisst unter allen
Umständen und zu jeder Zeit? Gibt es einen ganz wahrhaftigen Menschen
und kann es ihn gebe? (IX, 343, 4).

That this question aims at Rousseau's intent to show his fellowmen "un homme dans toute la vérité de la nature" (p. 5) appears
manifest; less so, however, is the implication of Keller's use of the
word *Kristall* in reference to literary and confessional truths—a
key word of Rousseau, who dreams of rendering his heart "transparent comme le cristal" (p. 446). Confiding to Judith, Heinrich
speaks a language that could be Jean-Jacques' own: ". . . ich
möchte für sie [Anna] ein braver und ehrenhafter Mann werden,
an welchem alles durch und durch rein und klar ist, dass sie mich
durchschauen dürfte wie einen Kristall . . ." (IV, 230).[27]

Related to the symbol of the crystal is that of the mirror as an
extension of the idea of the journal. The seventeen-year-old Keller
affirms: "Ein Mann ohne Tagebuch (habe er es im Kopf oder auf
Papier geschrieben) ist, was ein Weib ohne Spiegel" (XXI, 30). As
to whether introspection and self-knowledge are in themselves possible and worthwhile, Keller, in opposition to Goethe ("Inwendig
lernt kein Mensch sein Innerstes / Erkennen"),[28] tends to agree
with Rousseau, and at that, quite optimistically, without the latter's circumspection: "Ich habe zwar mir das ganze Bild in seinen
Umrissen und mit seinen Lokalfarben ziemlich treu bewahrt, und
wenn ich einst aus mir selbst heraustrete und als ein zweites Ich
mein ursprüngliches eignes Ich in seinem Herzkämmerlein auf-
stören und betrachten, wenn ich meine Jugendgeschichte schreiben
wollte, so würde mir dies, ungeachtet ich bis jetzt nie ein Tagebuch führte und nur früher, vor bereits sechs Jahren, dann und
wann, aber sehr selten, einzelne abgerissene Vorgänge der Aussen-
und Innenwelt aufzeichnete, dennoch ziemlich gelingen" (XXI,
34).

Admittedly, these are the beliefs of a young man—he was
twenty-two when he noted them—and perhaps because of it, they
ring true. As to the sense of these childhood reminiscences, Keller
leaves no doubt that they are meant to console him: "Der Haupt-
grund aber, der mich zur Führung eines solchen [Tagebuches]

trieb, liegt in der Beschäftigung an sich selber, die sie mir verleiht. Das Tagebuch wird mir ein Asyl sein für jene grauen, hoffnungslosen Tage, die mir oft in stumpfem Nichtstun vorübergehen und spurlos in die dämmernde Vergangenheit verschwinden" (XXI, 35). And he continues in a different key: "Ich will die schönsten Blüten erlebter Freude hineinlegen, wie die Kinder Rosen- und Tulpenblätter in ihre Gebetbücher legen; und wie sie sich dann in späteren Jahren wehmütig erfreuen, wann ihnen so ein verblichenes Blumenblatt in einem alten Buche zufällig wieder in die Hände fällt: so will ich mich in meinen letzten Erdentagen erfreuen an den Bildern entschwundener Freuden" (XXI, 37).

Here young Keller strikes an elegiac note characteristic of the old Rousseau: "Que j'aime à tomber de tems en tems sur les momens agréables de ma jeunesse? Ils m'étoient si doux; ils ont été si courts, si rares, et je les ai goûtés à si bon marché: Ah! leur seul souvenir rend encore à mon cœur une volupté pure dont j'ai besoin pour ranimer mon courage, et soutenir les ennuis du reste de mes ans" (pp. 134, 5).

But whereas Rousseau elegizes a life that he has lived, Keller elegizes for the sake of elegy. According to his own testimony, the first creative impulse regarding *Der grüne Heinrich* seems to have been released by a death-wish and related guilt feelings:

Allerlei erlebte Not und die Sorge, welche ich der Mutter bereitete, ohne dass ein gutes Ziel in Aussicht stand, beschäftigten meine Gedanken und mein Gewissen, bis sich die Grübelei in den Vorsatz verwandelte, einen traurigen kleinen Roman zu schreiben über den tragischen Abbruch einer jungen Künstlerlaufbahn, an welcher Mutter und Sohn zugrunde gingen. Dies war meines Wissens der erste schriftstellerische Vorsatz, den ich mit Bewusstsein gefasset habe, und ich war ungefähr dreiundzwanzig Jahre alt. Es schwebte mir das Bild eines elegisch-lyrischen Buches vor mit heiteren Episoden und einem zypressendunklen Schlusse, wo alles begraben wurde (XXI, 18).

It is known how stubbornly Keller clung to his death-ending for the second version of his novel, and one suspects that despite his Feuerbachian *Bejahung des Diesseits* and his Goethean "hingebende Liebe an alles Gewordene und Bestehende" (V, 4) Keller's "stille Grundtrauer,"[29] so pervasive in his poetry and prose, springs from a grief at having to live, while Jean-Jacques, champion of human happiness, regrets that his *bonheur* has had to pass and is no more.[30]

Contrary to Rousseau's *Confessions*, Keller's *Jugendgeschichte* is not exclusively grounded in an existential awareness of the *Moi seul,* but in a chthonic base: "Mein Vater war ein Bauernsohn aus einem uralten Dorfe . . ." (III, 1). His description of his ancestors, of the land where they lived, died, and were buried, as well as his short history of political and religious traditions, furnish a novelistic frame eminently suitable for the development of his epic autobiographical genius. Only towards the conclusion of the second chapter is there mention of himself in the first person singular: "Er liess seine Frau mit einem fünfjährigen Kinde allein zurück, und dies Kind bin ich" (III, 20). And from this point on, a reader steeped in the *Confessions* finds himself constantly reminded of Jean-Jacques' evocations. At times, the resemblance is purely affective, at other times, the analogies appear thematic, intellectual, and even stylistic. These points of congruence defy a systematic reduction into logical patterns, since both writers are concerned not with relating facts, but experiences, remembered and imagined. It could be argued that childhood experiences are by the nature of things similar and that tangential coincidences in Rousseau's and Keller's youths are not noteworthy. Such an objection may seem true if one forgets that the *Confessions* and *Der grüne Heinrich* are as much literature as they are life and that it was precisely one of Rousseau's great achievements to have transformed a hitherto neglected part of life into literature. In the words of Marcel Raymond: "Encore faudrait-il . . . rappeler que l'autobiographie de Rousseau a contribué au premier chef à transformer le concept même de littérature, centré désormais, non plus sur l'œuvre, être ou objet existant pour soi, mais sur l'auteur, et moins sur l'auteur que sur l'homme avec son drame personnel et sa figure irremplaçable."[31]

Indeed, one may almost be certain that Keller, before relating his *jeunesse romancée,* studied with creative intent the composition of great Western autobiographies, among them Rousseau's *Confessions.*[32] Like him, he avoids presenting a chronological sequence of experiences and events in favor of an order that respects the natural development of instincts, emotions, and concepts. A survey of the themes of the *Confessions* and of the first part of *Der grüne Heinrich* bears out this parallelism: we meet father and mother— in both cases, one of the parents dies, is eulogized, and the other, in spite of a remarriage, is idealized as well; then we are told of the growth of feelings, of the home, about books, pranks, God and the libido (in this matter, Keller skirts the issue), of fellowmen, cranks, school, injustice, apprenticeship, departure and the first encounter with a beautiful woman followed by the discovery of *le vert paradis des amours enfantines.* The mood of both narrators is one of serenity with elegiac overtones, although Jean-Jacques' account is at times saddened by tears occasioned by an involuntary memory which accuses and censures, but also enchants and revives. Elsewhere[33] I have tried to show to what degree the experience of time defines the life and thought of Jean-Jacques Rousseau. *Le temps vécu* is the very fabric of the *Confessions* which evoke all the dimensions of time—an uncertain future, a brittle present, or a captive past released by the sight of a *pervenche.* Gottfried Keller, however, unconsciously attracted by death, has to destroy time, which is not only the harbinger of death, but also the guarantor of life. I say unconsciously drawn to death or *Zeitlosigkeit,* for the conscious artist celebrates life, but in a *detemporalized* state; he often removes its tension, lets its blood, arrests its motion so that time becomes in the words of Emil Staiger "eine stehende Gegenwart": "Wir glauben nun das Wort zu verstehen, das Gottfried Keller am meisten eigentümlich ist und immer wiederkehrt: 'Ruhevoll.' 'Ruhevoll' blickt der grüne Heinrich Judiths 'Ruhe' an, 'ruhevoll' pflügen die Bauern in der stillen Septembergegend, 'ruhvoll' lehnt der Schiffer an dem Steuer."[34] And Staiger goes on to quote the celebrated passage:

Nur die Ruhe in der Bewegung hält die Welt und macht den Mann; die Welt ist innerlich ruhig und still, und so muss es auch der Mann sein, der sie verstehen und als ein wirkender Teil von ihr sie wiederspiegeln will. Ruhe zieht das Leben an, Unruhe verscheucht es; Gott hält sich mäuschenstill, darum bewegt sich die Welt um ihn. Für den künstlerischen Menschen nun wäre dies so anzuwenden, dass er sich eher leidend und zusehend verhalten und die Dinge an sich vorüberziehen lassen als ihnen nachjagen soll; denn wer in einem festlichen Zuge mitzieht, kann denselben nicht so beschreiben wie der, welcher am Wege steht (V, 5, 6).

Applied to autobiography and reduced *ad absurdum* this article of faith would seem to imply that an autobiographer cannot live if he wishes to tell his story: and this, in a sense, is precisely what happens to Heinrich Lee and Gottfried Keller. Yet, we only have to recall the turbulent lives of St. Augustine, Rousseau, Goethe, Gide, to realize that this sacrificial declaration represents not only a nineteenth-century opinion on the dilemma of the artist exemplified by Flaubert, but also the personal tragedy of Keller so well stated by Staiger: "Die Lebensgeschichte Heinrichs, seine grüne Torheit ist die Irrfahrt um die Ruhe im reinen Licht. Aber auch nachdem sie ihm erschienen und Gottfried Keller über ihr Wesen sich im klaren ist, kann er nicht bloss Auge sein und reinen Anschauns selig werden." "Die Unrast lockt nach wie vor . . ." And Staiger adds: "Denn der Lebensstrom ist eine unleugbare Wirklichkeit, als Segen mächtig wie als Fluch."[35] But, whenever possible, Keller avoids time or rather brings it to a halt: "Die Zeit geht nicht, sie stehet still" (I, 214). The temporal structure of his autobiographical novel reflects this need for arrestation. It is written for the most part in a quiescent past which one may contrast by way of illustration with Rousseau's past overflowing with desire, and its hero, Heinrich Lee, rarely if ever confronts a future iridescent like a summer day, a present that cuts to the quick, or a past that overwhelms like a wave. And, whenever possible, Keller, the magician, turns time into space to feast his eyes on what *is* from the viewpoint "eines Lebendig-Begrabenen" (XIV, 157 ff).

To put the matter into Kantian terms, one could affirm that Rousseau grants primacy to the *a priori* intuition of time whereas Keller subordinates time to the *a priori* intuition of space. As a result of this intuitive differential and ensuing stylistic changes, their visions of their *home* (that is to say, that garden, room, corner, or attic that *was* home in our childhood) appear different in terms of what is being described, although these visions do not *feel* different in terms of the general impression they produce—at least, on this reader's imagination. The answer to this puzzle may be that far more important than their *Raum-* or *Zeiterlebnis* is their immense yearning for an ideal home they never knew. "Dans la maison qui n'est plus," writes Gaston Bachelard, "nous aimons vivre encore parce que nous y revivons, souvent sans nous en bien rendre compte, une dynamique du réconfort."[36] Here is a well-known recollection by Rousseau of which the final version was drafted in Wooton, England:

Près de trente ans se sont passés depuis ma sortie de Bossey sans que je m'en sois rappelé le séjour d'une manière agréable par des souvenirs un peu liés: mais depuis qu'ayant passé l'âge mur je décline vers la vieillesse, je sens que ces mêmes souvenirs renaissent tandis que les autres s'effacent, et se gravent dans ma mémoire avec des traits dont le charme et la force augmentent de jour en jour; comme si, sentant déjà la vie qui s'échappe, je cherchois à la ressaisir par ces commencemens. Les moindres faits de ce tems-là me plaisent par cela seul qu'ils sont de ce tems-là. Je me rappelle toutes les circonstances des lieux, des personnes, des heures. Je vois la servante ou le valet agissant dans la chambre, une hirondelle entrant par la fenêtre, une mouche se poser sur ma main, tandis que je récitois ma leçon: je vois tout l'arrangement de la chambre où nous étions; le cabinet de M. Lambercier à main droite, une estampe réprésentant tous les papes, un barometre, un grand calendrier; des framboisiers qui, d'un jardin élevé dans lequel la maison s'enfonçoit sur le derriére, venoient ombrager la fenêtre, et passoient quelquefois jusqu'en dedans (p. 21).

Unlike Keller, who draws his perspectives in space, Rousseau creates his perspective in time, achieving contrapuntal effects by contrasting the lessening number of years to live with the increasing meaning of his remembrances. Throughout the passage, Rousseau maintains an equilibrium between past and present that reminds one of St. Augustine's "praesens de praeteritis."[37] Gradually his reminiscences find their liberation; at last they blossom, and the shapes and sounds of a long lost day become real once more.

But let us compare his autobiographical visions to Keller's narrative about his younger days:

Den Tag über betrachtete ich stundenlang das innere häusliche Leben in diesen Höfen; die grünen Gärtchen in denselben schienen mir kleine Paradiese zu sein, wenn die Nachmittagssonne sie beleuchtete und die weisse Wäsche darin sanft flatterte, und wunderfremd und doch bekannt kamen mir die Leute vor, welche ich fern gesehen hatte, wenn sie plötzlich einmal in unsrer Stube standen und mit der Mutter plauderten. Unser eigenes Höfchen enthielt zwischen hohen Mauern ein ganz kleines Stückchen Rasen mit zwei Vogelbeerbäumchen; ein nimmermüdes Brünnchen ergoss sich in ein ganz grün gewordenes Sandsteinbecken, und der enge Winkel ist kühl und fast schauerlich, ausgenommen im Sommer, wo die Sonne täglich einige Stunden darin ruht. Alsdann schimmert das verborgene Grün durch den dunklen Hausflur so kokett auf die Gasse, wenn die Haustür aufgeht, dass den Vorübergehenden immer eine Art Gartenheimweh befällt. Im Herbst werden diese Sonnenblicke kürzer und milder, und wenn dann die Blätter an den zwei Bäumchen gelb und die Beeren brennend rot werden, die alten Mauern so wehmütig vergoldet sind und das Wässerchen einigen Silberglanz dazu gibt, so hat dieser kleine abgeschiedene Raum einen so wunderbar melancholischen Reiz, dass er dem Gemüte ein Genüge tut wie die weiteste Landschaft (III, 26, 7).

While Rousseau's passage resounds with the music of his language—it is almost a *poème en prose*—Keller's narrative vibrates with colors. Rousseau sings, Keller paints;[38] the former journeys through time, the latter moves within space or *Räumlichkeit,* as Stifter would have it. Rousseau, the man, is omnipresent, whereas Keller sacrifices his immediate presence to that of a child gazing at shapes near and far. To my way of feeling, *die sanft flatternde Wäsche* is a touch of genius. Who of the pre-war generation does not recall his childish fascination with white fluttering laundry shimmering with colors as on a canvas by Utrillo? Rousseau's mood is calm, whereas Keller's *Stimmung* is autumnal suggesting a vision of children and old people in deserted squares. . . .

Yet, despite these differences of approach, treatment, language and literary periods—is Rousseau not the greatest pre-romantic lyrical realist and Keller not the greatest post-romantic lyrical realist of European literature?—the citizen of Geneva and the *Staatsschreiber* share an abiding love of childhood appreciated for its own sake. Where, if not in the *Confessions,* was Keller to have found a model, an inspiration for his *Jugendgeschichte?* Neither classical nor Italian nor Spanish literature could offer him examples of autobiographical childhood evocations that are tender, realistic, and lyrical. Blake and Wordsworth were unknown to him, and as far as German literature is concerned, neither Jung-Stilling's *Leben,* pious and awkward, nor Moritz's *Anton Reiser,* analytical and hysterical, nor Goethe's *Dichtung und Wahrheit,* fits his views and concepts. Aside from Jean-Jacques, there remains as the only other source the inimitable *Professor der Selbstgeschichte* whose *Selberlebensbeschreibung* features passages so suggestive of the *Confessions* and *Der grüne Heinrich* that they create the uneasy and illogical impression of being a composite pastiche of Rousseau and Keller done by Jean Paul—for instance, this fragment by Germany's greatest humorist: "Ich bin zu meiner Freude imstande, aus meinem zwölf-, wenigstens vierzehnmonatlichen Alter eine bleiche kleine Erinnerung, gleichsam das erste geistige Schneeglöckchen aus dem dunkeln Erdboden der Kindheit noch aufzuheben. Ich erinnere mich nämlich noch, dass ein armer Schüler mich sehr liebgehabt und ich ihn und dass er mich immer auf den Armen—was angenehmer ist als oft später auf den Händen—getragen . . . Sein fernes nachdunkelndes Bild und sein Lieben schwebte mir über spätere Jahre herein; leider weiss ich seinen Namen längst nicht mehr . . ."[39]

But let us focus on specific episodic resemblances between the *Confessions* and *Der grüne Heinrich.* Of the many, only three have been studied and these by Cornicelius and Faulkner; the former establishing an analogy between the *petit ruban rose* and the *Kinderverbrechen* as well as between Jean-Jacques' abandonment of M. Le Maitre and Heinrich's cruel treatment of Römer, the latter dovetailing Mlles Goton and de Vulson with Judith and Anna. Cornicelius begins his article, whose implications have been steadfastly ignored by Keller's critics, with a reminder as to the need of textual comparisons: "Die einzige unbedingt sichere und zuverlässige Grundlage für die Untersuchung bieten allein seine Werke. Aber so sicher dieser Grund daliegt, dennoch lässt sich hier bei Dichtern, die, wie Gottfried Keller, nur das in sich aufnehmen, was sie sich völlig zu eigen machen können, Angeborenes und Angeeignetes nicht immer leicht unterscheiden."[40] He then proceeds to summarize these celebrated crimes and concludes on the basis of Keller's declaration that he had lied to do justice to the "poetische Gerechtigkeit [seiner] Erfindung": "Es handelt sich also hier bei Keller, im Unterschied von dem, was Rousseau von sich bekennt, um ein Vergehen, das aus dem Kopfe, nicht aus dem Herzen entsprungen ist . . ."[41]

For my part, I suspect that the fictitious story of obscene words exchanged in the *Brüderleinholz* masks a libidinous experience far more likely to have occurred than the supposed desire of a six-year-old to do poetic justice to his creative powers. The second analogy studied by Cornicelius compares Rousseau's abandonment of M. Le Maitre ill with epilepsy in Lyon and the story of Römer whose destiny took a turn for the worse because of a letter sent by Heinrich—a letter composed by Keller's mother and never sent. The parallel is striking, especially if one considers the fact that the betrayal never happened and that Keller availed himself of the Rousseauean pattern to mask once more the loss of what Judith calls his "moralische Jungfernschaft" (V, 68) occasioned by guilt feelings of whose origins we know nothing.

Before tracing Rousseau's influence on Keller's views on women, it would be well to compare their attitudes on love. Many of Jean-Jacques' exclamations seem almost predestined for Keller: "J'ai ainsi passé ma vie à convoiter et me taire auprès des personnes que j'aimois le plus" (p. 17) or "J'ai donc fort peu possédé, mais je n'ai pas laissé de jouir beaucoup à ma maniére, c'est-à-dire, par l'imagination" (p. 17). Because of choice or necessity, both men came to assume a point of view that stresses adoration instead of possession. They are artists who dare not, will not, cannot sacrifice their respective identities for the sake of love and who call upon their creative powers to fill the ensuing void in their lives.[42] Rousseau's celebrated letter to Malesherbes relates an *état d'âme* that might well have been Keller's own after suffering so many dis-

appointments: "Mon imagination ne laissoit pas longtemps déserte
la terre ainsi parée. Je la peuplois bientôt d'êtres selon mon cœur,
et chassant bien loin l'opinion, les prejugés, toutes les passions
factices, je transportois dans les asiles de la nature des hommes
dignes de les habiter . . . Je me faisois un siècle d'or à ma fantaisie,
et remplissant ces beaux jours de toutes les scènes de ma vie qui
m'avoient laissé de doux souvenirs, et de toutes celles que mon
cœur pouvoit désirer encore, je m'attendrissois jusqu'aux larmes
sur les vrais plaisirs de l'humanité . . ."[43]

Admittedly, there is a difference between regretting a Mme
d'Houdetot one has known, and a Judith one has imagined. Rousseau's life was much richer in love than Keller's, who never knew
a *Maman* or a Mme de Larnage. Yet, despite these and many other
experiential differences, both writers emphasize or create situations
in which their young heroes find themselves caught in a web of
desire and fear like Jean-Jacques at the feet of Mme Basile or
Heinrich between Judith and Anna. Their women tend to be
strong and protective towards their lovers, who seek to escape their
responsibilities.[44] But whereas Keller condemns his anti-hero to
erotic inaction, Jean-Jacques succeeds in breaking the spell, although the rewards of self-knowledge may be painful: "J'étois
comme si j'avois commis un inceste" (p. 197). Heinrich's withdrawal from Judith may be explicable in terms of his or Keller's
neuroses, but from the viewpoint of the novel or autobiography
his departure from Judith lacks *vraisemblance* because Keller cannot or will not furnish convincing motives. Unlike Rousseau,
Keller does not "go all the way" in his childhood analysis, preferring seemingly the Goethean approach, without however being
able to justify this method by virtue of later achievements that
could reflect and explain his life. Rousseau's account of his *liaison*
with Mme de Warens approaches truth not only because it happened but because he is able to synthesize the demands of art with
the facts of his life. Whatever critics may think of the *Confessions*,
few would deny that they lack the "courage of being" and however much they may love Keller's magnificent tapestries, few have
experienced a sense of complete satisfaction upon reading the last
chapters of *Der grüne Heinrich*. Neither his *mise à mort* of the
first version nor the *dea ex America* ending of the second version
is convincing. It is better to stop abruptly like Stendhal, who discovered a successful way of not ending his autobiography and
novels, then to keep on writing like Keller, whose final chapters

tend to be pompous. Furthermore, Keller's wordiness impairs his *sententiae*. They lack the inner resonance and tension of Rousseau's and Nietzsche's aphorisms. For the most part objective, his *Lebensweisheiten* have an Emersonian ring and lend themselves to adorning Swiss calendars for the edification of unrepentant sons and husbands. . . .

"Je connois deux sortes d'amours très distincts, très réels," confides Rousseau, "et qui n'ont presque rien de commun, quoique très vifs l'un et l'autre, et tous deux differens de la tendre amitié. Tout le cours de ma vie s'est partagé entre ces deux amours de si diverses natures, et je les ai même éprouvés tous deux à la fois . . ." (p. 27). Basing his belief on this remark and the ensuing disquisition on Mlle Goton and Mlle de Vulson, Faulkner concluded as early as 1912 that there is "strong circumstantial evidence to something more than the general influence of the *Confessions* which Keller admitted of his autobiographical novel" and that "the incident of Mesdemoiselles de Vulson and Goton" constitutes "the framework about which Keller constructed the double-love story of Judith and Anna, though there is no reference to his indebtedness either in Bächthold's biography or in Keller's published correspondence and diary."[45] This viewpoint has prevailed in criticism and as late as 1950, Ermatinger does little but restate it:

Im *Grünen Heinrich* hat Keller diesem rousseauisch-romantischen Motive der Doppelliebe in Heinrichs Verhältnis zu Anna und Judith eine bedeutsame Vertiefung und Ausweitung gegeben. Wenn auf den zwölf-jährigen Rousseau die Liebkosungen der zwanzigjährigen Freundin keinen sinnlichen Reiz üben . . . so scheidet Keller, der Feuerbachschüler, Heinrichs Liebe zu Judith scharf von der zu Anna. An dieser hängt seine Geistigkeit, nach jener drängen seine Sinne, und indem die Neigung zu Anna mit dieser stirbt und Judith zu gleicher Zeit immer mehr Gewalt über den Jüngling bekommt, erscheint diese Doppelliebe als Offenbarung eines geheimnisvollen Naturgeschehens—des allmählichen Sieges der Sinnlichkeit über schwärmerische Geistigkeit.[46]

If it is true that this is the extent of Rousseau's influence on Keller, it follows that his critics have never read beyond the first book of the *Confessions*. If they had, they would have encountered Mme de Warens, the acknowledged ancestor of *la femme de trente ans,* from Mme de Rênal to Mme de Mortsauf, including the magnificent Judith of the original version, who happens to be in her thirties during her first meeting with Heinrich. But this is not all. In the eleventh chapter, entitled "Theatergeschichten—

Gretchen und die Meerkatze," Heinrich Lee finds himself in the enviable situation of being caught by Gretchen. A juxtaposition of Rousseau's first meeting with Mme de Warens and Heinrich's encounter with the actress discloses surprising and delightful similarities:

Prette à entrer dans cette porte, Mad^e de Warens se retourne à ma voix. Que devins-je à cette vue! Je m'étois figuré une vieille dévote bien rechignée: la bonne Dame de M. de Pontverre ne pouvoit être autre chose à mon avis. Je vois un visage pétri de grâces, de beaux yeux bleus pleins de douceur, un teint éblouissant, le contour d'une gorge enchanteresse. Rien n'échappa au rapide coup d'œil du jeune prosélyte; car je devins à l'instant le sien; sûr qu'une réligion prêchée par de tels missionnaires ne pouvoit manquer de mener en paradis. Elle prend en souriant la lettre que je lui présente d'une main tremblante, l'ouvre, jette un coup d'œil sur celle de M. de Pontverre, revient à la mienne qu'elle lit toute entiére, et qu'elle eût relue encore, si son laquais ne l'eût avertie qu'il étoit tems d'entrer. Eh! mon enfant, me dit-elle d'un ton qui me fit tressaillir, vous voilà courant le pays bien jeune; c'est dommage en vérité. Puis sans attendre ma réponse, elle ajoûta: allez chez moi m'attendre; dites qu'on vous donne à déjeuner: après la messe j'irai causer avec vous (p. 49).

Da trat sie auf mich zu, streifte meine Maske zurück, fasste mein Gesicht zwischen ihre Hände und rief, indem sie laut lachte: "Herr Gott! das ist die aufmerksame Meerkatze! Ei, du kleiner Schalk! bist du es, der den Lärm gemacht hat, als ob ein Gewitter im Hause wäre?"—"Ja!" sagte ich, indem meine Augen fortwährend auf dem weissen Raume ihrer Brust hafteten und mein Herz zum ersten Male wieder so andächtig erfreut war wie einst, wenn ich in das glänzende Feld des Abendrotes geschaut und den lieben Gott darin geahnt hatte. Dann betrachtete ich in vollkommener Ruhe ihr schönes Gesicht und gab mich unbefangen dem süssen Eindrucke ihres reizenden Mundes hin. Sie sah mich eine Weile still und ernsthaft an, dann sprach sie: "Mich dünkt, du bist ein guter Junge; doch wenn du einst gross geworden, wirst du ein Lümmel sein wie alle!" Und hiermit schloss sie mich an sich und küsste mich mehrere Male auf meinen Mund, der nur dadurch leise bewegt wurde, dass ich heimlich, von ihren Küssen unterbrochen, ein herzliches Dankgebet an Gott richtete für das herrliche Abenteuer.

Hierauf sagte sie: "Es ist nun am besten, du bleibest bei mir, bis es Tag ist; denn Mitternacht ist längst vorüber" (III, 128).

Both passages begin with a surprise: Jean-Jacques expecting "une vieille dévote bien rechignée," Heinrich a ghost. Both boys are fascinated respectively by "le contour d'une gorge enchanteresse" and von "dem weissen Raume ihrer Brust," and considering the matter historically, it should not be too difficult for a *comparatiste* to appreciate the neoclassical outlines of Rousseau's phrase as opposed to the more spatial view of Keller so characteristic of nineteenth century literature and painting. That each youth enjoys a vision of paradise or God seems more than a coincidence. The mood is identical—ironic, witty, tender. The actress, no less than Mme de Warens, appears to be beautiful and, secretly charmed, offers a haven as well as well as promise of happiness.

But there is a difference. Rousseau's adventure happened in the sunlight of Palm Sunday in 1728, and in 1778 the last lines he ever wrote recall that day: "Aujourdui jour de paques fleuries il y a precisement cinquante ans de ma prémiére connoissance avec Mad^e de Warens."[47] Heinrich's adventure occurs at night, and the actress' words: "Es ist nun am besten Du bleibst bei mir bis es Tag ist . . ." reveal only too clearly that she was but a post-romantic dream to Gottfried Keller, in whose life love and destiny would not meet.

Let us return to Judith. In the words of Keller, "eine Naturmanifestation,"[48] she is a character unlike any of Rousseau's contemporaries or creations. Nonetheless, "die reizende Pomona" appears in a scene whose thematic structure and treatment show a marked resemblance to the conclusion of Rousseau's *Idylle des Cerises* studied in the second chapter. It tells how he spends a summer day in the company of chance-acquaintances: Mlle Galley and Mlle de Graffenried. Their pleasures are few and harmless. They ride on horseback, have a pique-nique, accept a handkiss: ". . . nous nous aimions sans mistère et sans honte, et nous voulions nous aimer toujours ainsi" (p. 138). At one point, Jean-Jacques climbs a cherry tree just as Judith ascends an apple tree, and a comparison of texts reveals other analogies:

Je montai sur l'arbre et je leur en jettois des bouquets dont elles me rendoient les noyaux à travers les branches. Une fois Mlle Galley avançant son tablier et reculant la tête se présentoit si bien, et je visai si juste, que je luis fis tomber un bouquet dans le sein; et de rire. Je me disois en moi-même; que mes levres ne sont-elles des cérises! comme je les leur jetterois ainsi de bon cœur! (p. 137)

Sie ging mir voran zu einem Baume, dessen Äste und Blätter edler gebaut schienen, als die der übrigen, stieg auf einer Leiter einige Sprossen hinan und brach einige schön geformte und gefärbte Äpfel. Einen davon, der noch im feuchten Dufte glänzte, biss sie mit ihren weissen Zähnen entzwei, gab mir die abgebissene Hälfte und fing an, die andere zu essen. Ich ass die meinige ebenfalls und rasch; sie war von der seltensten Frische und Gewürzigkeit, und ich konnte kaum erwarten, bis sie es mit dem zweiten Apfel ebenso machte. Als wir drei Früchte so gegessen, war mein Mund so süss erfrischt, dass ich mich zwingen musste, Judith nicht zu küssen und die Süsse von ihrem Munde noch dazu zu nehmen (V, 39).

Both scenes derive from the pastoral ideal whose antecedents are Christian and classical, Christian because the settings recall the Garden of Eden and the Tree of Knowledge; classical, since the European pastoral has always been dominated by Graeco-Latin and Italian ideals (from Theocritus to Tasso and Milton). Keller's references to Paradise are direct: the branches and leaves of the tree appear "edler" and the taste of its fruit "von seltenster Frische und Gewürzigkeit." These attributes suggest a conscious elaboration of pre-existing models among which figures quite probably Rousseau's *Idylle*. His language seems simpler, more transparent than Keller's whose stylized slow-motion effect reveals Goethean influences. Common to both passages is an impression of freshness as well as of harmony between fruit and kiss:

> Comme le fruit se fond en jouissance
> . . .
> Dans une bouche où sa forme se meurt . . . (Valéry)

Even the sounds suggest subtle affinities that should be studied according to the laws of *la phonétique sensuelle;* for instance, the sibilants and labials in the exclamation "que mes levres ne sont-elles des cérises [sic]!" harmonize quite gracefully with their German counterparts: "Als wir drei Früchte so gegessen, war mein Mund so süss erfrischt, dass ich mich zwingen musste, Judith nicht zu küssen und die Süsse von ihrem Munde noch dazu zu neh-men."[49]

Keller's stated views on the idyll are somewhat misleading. In chapter xx, entitled "Berufsahnungen," he tells of his enthusiastic discovery of Gessner's treatise on landscape painting: "Ich liebte sogleich diesen Mann und machte ihn zu meinem Propheten" (III, 224).[50] After identifying himself with Gessner for having been a hopeless student, Keller engages in a curious discussion on the difference between authentic and inauthentic genius, implying that a genius is not unlike the fox that covers his footprints and notes: "Ja, es ist überhaupt die Frage, ob nicht zu dem bescheidensten Gelingen eine dichte Unterlage von bewussten Vorsätzen und allem Apparate der Geniesucht gehöre, und der Unterschied mag oft nur darin bestehen, dass das wirkliche Genie diesen Apparat

nicht sehen lässt, sondern vorweg verbrennt . . ." (III, 225). In the
next paragraph, he resumes his discussion of Gessner, although it
is unclear whether he refers to Gessner the painter or the author
of the *Idyllen:* "Den berückenden Trank schöpfte ich jedoch nicht
aus einem anspruchsvollen und blendenden Zauberbecher, sondern aus einer bescheidenen lieblichen Hirtenschale . . ." (III, 225).
However, the title of the following chapter "Sonntagsidylle—Der
Schulmeister und sein Kind" instead of pursuing the themes of
Gessner, points unmistakably to Jean Paul, the theoretician of the
modern idyll, and, indirectly, to Rousseau, its creator. Furthermore, a scene in "Der Landvogt von Greifensee" shows Keller
quite knowledgeable on some of the finer points of the history of
the idyll.[51] Here, his treatment of Rousseau is characteristic.
Owing him so much, he projects Rousseau into the background of
this discussion of idylls to have him assume the stereotypical rôle
of the *Schwärmer für den idealen Naturzustand*—an attitude,
Keller knew, bearing no relation to Rousseau's real function in
European letters. In the second chapter, I have tried to clarify
aspects of this function which relate to the genesis of the modern
idyll or pastoral by showing that *l'Idylle des Cerises* represents a
metamorphosis of the classical pastoral ideal derived from Theocritus and Virgil, and that Schiller in his *Über naive und sentimentalische Dichtung* and Jean Paul in his *Aesthetische Vorschule*
attempted to formulate theories capable of sustaining a modern
idyll. However much Keller may have admired Schiller, his tem-
perament and the age he lived in prevented him from executing
Schiller's exhortations to the modern poet to take upon himself
"die Aufgabe einer Idylle, welche jene Hirtenunschuld auch in
Subjekten der Kultur und unter allen Bedingungen des rüstigsten
feurigsten Lebens, des ausgebreitetsten Denkens, der raffiniertesten
Kunst, der höchsten gesellschaftlichen Verfeinerung ausführt,
welche, mit einem Wort, den Menschen, der nun einmal nicht
mehr nach *Arkadien* zurück kann, bis nach Elysium führt."[52] Far
more suited to Keller's genius and personal inclinations must have
been Jean Paul's considerations on the idyll which he defines as
the "epische Darstellung des Vollglücks in der Beschränkung"[53]—
a brilliant definition that applies also to Judith (Is she not *ein
Vollweib in der Beschränkung?*).

With these ideas in mind, chapters like "Sonntagsidylle," "Die
Bohnenromanze," and "Judith" assume a new dimension in the
perspective of literary history. They exemplify Rousseau's direct
influence as in the case of *l'Idylle des Cerises* and his indirect

influence through Jean Paul who, by example and theory, must himself have played an important rôle in the conception and execution of some of Keller's finest passages. They testify to Keller's undisputed mastery of what one might call *die episch-lyrische Stimmung*. No nineteenth century author with the possible exception of Stifter achieves such a smooth reconciliation of the conflicting demands of the pastoral, the novel, and the autobiography, and it is only with the advent of Marcel Proust that we encounter an artist capable of harmonizing the ancient strain of the pastoral flute with the music within ourselves and those whom we imagine and love.

In an essay that has become well known, Friedrich Theodor Vischer wrote about Keller's portrait of his paternal grandmother: ". . . wer dieses Bild gezeichnet, versteht es . . . um das Lebenswahre den Schleier zu ziehen, der ihm den Zauber des ahnungsvollen Traumes gibt."[54] One is tempted to apply this remark with appropriate modifications to Keller's use of his source material, over which he casts a veil, transforming whatever he may have borrowed into the most intimate of intuitions. Perhaps it is more fitting to suggest that he borrowed only what he could incorporate into his own design. Too intelligent to deny his boyhood infatuation with Jean Paul and too much of an autodidact to resist the temptation to regale his readers with chips of erudition about Rousseau, Gottfried Keller, already successful, mentions their names, it would seem, *à contre cœur* and sometimes *à contre temps*. We have seen how loftily he dismisses Rousseau's immense influence,[55] attested by prominent Germans from Kant to Cassirer, from Goethe to Thomas Mann, to a mere breath of his "konfessionelle Herbigkeit." Similarly, in the second version of *Der grüne Heinrich*, he reduces his laudatory remarks on Jean Paul by over a half, declaring à propos to Frey: "Es gab eine Zeit, wo ich selten einschlief, ohne Jean Pauls Werke unter dem Kopfkissen zu haben. Aber in jenen späten Tagen, da ich zu schreiben anfing, tat ich längst keinen Blick mehr in seine Schriften, und von einer Wirkung auf meine Produktion kann daher in der von einigen Literarhistorikern angenommenen Weise keine Rede sein."[56] These and other refusals of the aging Keller to admit to any influence other than Goethe's do not diminish his greatness. However, they grant us an insight into why he wrote and, by extension, into the relationship between the *Confessions* and *Der grüne Heinrich*.

Resorting to simplification, one is tempted to claim that Rousseau wants to know *who* he is and *what* he is. To Jean-Jacques, writing is a means to an end. His *Confessions* and other works bear witness to his power to transcend literature and his reader is, like Pascal, ". . . tout étonné, car on s'attendait de voir un auteur, et on trouve un homme." Keller, on the other hand, is more concerned with knowing *that* he is and what he *ought* to be. This distinction, however tenuous and relative, strikes me as one of the lessons of this confrontation; it may account perhaps for Keller's surly insistence on his literary originality, since what he wrote came to be a surrogate of his existence.[57] This, at least, seems likely in regard to *Der grüne Heinrich* in which, unwilling to wager his life, Keller offers his readers and himself a literary facsimile of his aspirations, dreams, and failures, rather than an authentic projection of his self.[58]

Rousseau also writes to console himself and expiates, like Keller, the death of his parent. But, whereas Heinrich Lee appears incapable of ever leaving the realm of his mother, Jean-Jacques abandons personal guilt to struggle against original sin, declaring himself to be good by nature, by volition—by virtue of his life. This is the deeper sense of *l'Idylle des Charmettes* in which Rousseau swears to have known happiness by, and within, himself without seeking help from anyone or anything—God, science, or society: "Ici commence le court bonheur de ma vie; ici viennent les paisibles mais rapides momens qui m'ont donné le droit de dire que j'ai vécu" (p. 225).[59] It is inconceivable that *Der grüne Heinrich* could have been written without sustenance and encouragement from such powerful affirmations. Yet, many of Gottfried Keller's beliefs and axioms oppose the *Confessions,* the most important of these being a conviction characteristic of most *Bildungsromane,* the insistence on public service and the renunciation for its sake, of all personal dreams: *hors du bureau, point de salut.* Another axiom, more terrible still, is uttered by Vater Jakoblein who, wracked by pain and old age, goes about shouting: ". . . man sollte die Menschen totschlagen, ehe sie so alt und elend würden" (III, 87).

Thus, if by way of conclusion, one had to trace human discrepancies between Rousseau's *Confessions* and Keller's *Der grüne Heinrich,* it would have to be in areas as ambiguous as those of sacrifice and public self-immolation—in fields of tension between duty towards oneself and duty towards others. But who can tell the measure of love?—the difference between *entsagen*[60] and *versagen?*

CHAPTER V

Rousseau and Thoreau

Wir säuseln, wir rieseln
Wir flüstern Dir zu. (*Faust*)

Individualists *à outrance,* both are related to Romanticism: Jean-Jacques Rousseau being the father of the new world, Thoreau one of its sons. Their relationship is strengthened by affinities, not only in ideas, but also in their lives which are the very fabric of their works sustained by their power of self-analysis. Solitary figures, forever deprived of the comfort of agreement and the pleasures of acquiescence, their characters stand in sharp contrast to those of their respective contemporaries. The outlines of their psyches are hence distinct and this clarity, intensified by the power of their insight, enables us to discern their tragic quest to be their own redeemers. Indeed, both men make the principle *Know thyself* the indispensable premise of their lives and their words. Thus, Rousseau declares at the outset of his *Confessions* that he wishes to show himself "dans toute la vérité de la nature," and that no one had ever undertaken such an enterprise. Despite his seeming vanity, he may have been right, for the great autobiographers that precede him do not reach his level of existential self-awareness. St. Augustine's *Confessions* view life as a journey that leads to the *City of God* and Montaigne, while admirably subtle and self-objective, does not study himself in depth. Similarly, Thoreau requires ". . . of every writer, first or last, a simple and sincere account of his own life . . ."[1] a demand certain to raise suspicion in the minds of wary critics. I think that both men were honest men, and few scholars, well acquainted with their works and the excruciating complications and snares of autobiography, would accuse them of deliberate falsehood. Either may have been guilty of self-deception if one applies to his writing metaphysical and psychoanalytical criteria. Yet, do such criteria not consist of hypothetical constructs and do we not know more than we are able to define? Moreover, *la chasse aux âmes* is good sport, and if literary criticism is the all too human art of having to take a man at his word while having to suspect him, the reading of Rousseau and Thoreau is healthy exercise.

An interpretation of Rousseau's controversial life and work is further complicated by simplifications and prejudice. Many speak of him, but few have read him carefully. Scholars of American literature, in particular, have often dismissed Rousseau with thoughtless references to tearful and obscene sentimentality, a blithe return to nature, and political theories suggestive of fascism. Witness Harding's *A Thoreau Handbook* where he states that there is no evidence that Thoreau ever read Rousseau and then supposes that "Thoreau was undoubtedly repelled by Rousseau's moral laxity."[2] To emphasize this hypothesis, his handbook quotes a definitive statement by the Reverend Sylvester Smith: "Thoreau's thinking is clear enough. He believed in God; he believed in man . . ."[3]

To be sure, a historian such as Parrington has strongly insisted on Jean-Jacques' powerful influence in the development of the American Renaissance. But even he restricts this influence to the realm of emotions and does not draw the obvious conclusion that given the fact that Kant, Fichte, Hegel, and Schleiermacher were deeply indebted to Rousseau, the Transcendentalists, in turn indebted to the Germans, owe many ideas and feelings to the Citizen of Geneva. Thus, even a cursory survey of New England Transcendentalism reveals that many of its characteristics bear the imprint of Rousseau's mind and personality. In his lecture on Transcendentalism of 1842, Emerson insists on the subjectivity of the doctrine and goes on to state that the Transcendentalist "believes in the perpetual openness of the human mind to new influx of light and power [as well as] in inspiration and ecstasy."[4] Like Rousseau, the movement asserted the inalienable worth of man and sought to transfer supernatural attributes to the nature of man. Furthermore, writes Frothingham: ". . . while Transcendentalism is usually spoken of as a philosophy, it is more justly regarded as a gospel . . ."[5] and it is this fervor which is so reminiscent of Rousseau whose doctrines are often sustained by similar feelings, that is to say ". . . an enthusiasm, a wave of sentiment, a breadth of mind that caught up such as were prepared to receive it, elated them, transported them, and passed on,—no man knowing whither it went."[6] Following the example of Jean-Jacques, the

Transcendentalists insisted on challenge and redefinition of hallowed values—according to Parker, its main effort was "no less than this, to revise the experience of mankind and try its teachings by the nature of mankind [one thinks of the *Emile*]; to test ethics by conscience . . ."[7]

Unitarianism, which paralleled the transcendental movement, also reflects orthodox Rousseauean thought. Thus, Channing's doctrine, which asserted man's moral nature as being guided by instinct with divinity, echoes *La profession de foi du vicaire savoyard*, Schleiermacher's theology being the sounding board: "Conscience! conscience! instinct divin, immortelle et céleste voix, guide assuré d'un être ignorant et borné, mais intelligent et libre; juge infaillible du bien et du mal, qui rends l'homme semblable à Dieu; c'est toi qui fais l'excellence de sa nature et la moralité de ses actions . . ." (IV, 600, 1). And when one reads Dr. Channing's pious contemplations of the order and majesty of the cosmos as being the source of his consciousness of his fusion and oneness with the infinite, one is reminded of young Jean-Jacques praying in an orchard, waiting for *Maman's* shutters to open: "Là tout en me promenant je faisois ma priére, qui ne consistoit pas en un vain balbutiement de levres, mais dans une sincére elévation de cœur à l'auteur de cette aimable nature dont les beautés étoient sous mes yeux. Je n'ai jamais aimé à prier dans la chambre . . . J'aime à le [Dieu] contempler dans ses œuvres tandis que mon cœur s'élève à lui . . ." (I, 236).

To what degree Thoreau absorbed Transcendentalist ideas (that is, without his realizing it, Rousseau's ideas) is a question not easily resolved. Pochmann states the problem in his excellent *German Culture in America*: "For one thing, his deep-seated desire to be utterly himself and his horror of dependence make the attempt to find the sources of Thoreau a baffling process. Sharing the Transcendentalists' worship of self-trust and originality, he yet absorbed from them much of their enthusiasm for books from many lands. They were constantly putting books into each other's hands."[8] And because of the well-nigh impossibility of comparing the two men in the tarnished mirrors of *Geistesgeschichte* and histories of philosophy and religion, it may be best to compare the structure of their aspirations which both laid bare with alike cunning and innocence.

Especially valuable for understanding Rousseau's psyche are the *Confessions* and *Les rêveries du promeneur solitaire*. These autobiographical works, characterized by his wish to be the savior of his own soul, are from an artistic point of view his masterpieces. The former are unique in that they seek a justification of life in human terms with negligible recourse to transcendental agents and in this respect parallel the hopes and aspirations of Thoreau; the latter attempt to avoid anguish by overcoming dispersion in time in order to concentrate all being in the pure present. This struggle against disintegration and need of concentration constitute, as it were, the axis of Rousseau's contradiction. His soul is forever threatened to be torn into two parts. Like Hegel's Contrite Consciousness, he is desirous of being one while being tempted by two opposing ideals of unity; he has two goals of life which defeat one another.

The first one is the conquest of the present; it is an attempt *to be* and *to be aware of being*. Like Thoreau, he yearns to reach that state in which one enjoys existence for its own sake: "De quoi jouit-on dans une pareille situation? De rien d'extérieur à soi, de rien sinon de soi-même et de sa propre existence, tant que cet état dure on se suffit à soi-même comme Dieu" (I, 1047). God is conscious of all that is, and it is Rousseau's anxious desire to know this non-mediated awareness of life's plenitude. These attempts at self-possession alternate with cravings to become one with nature, by achieving the transparency of space and the fluidity of water. This twofold quest for divine self-sufficiency and pantheistic passivity takes place in the pure and eternal present and there is no need of past and future.

Rousseau's second goal of life takes place in the past and future, while the present, formerly the dimension of fulfillment, is now a dimension of sorrow and destruction. Every day that he lives sunders a spiritual and moral unity which Rousseau never experiences directly, but whose reality he divines with ardor and faith in order to endure the disintegration of his temporal existence: "J'aspire au moment où, délivré des entraves du corps, je serai *moi* sans contradiction, sans partage, et n'aurai besoin que de moi pour être heureux: en attendant je le suis dès cette vie, parce que j'en compte pour peu tous les maux, que je la regarde comme presque étrangére à mon être" (IV, 604, 5). Now, Rousseau's past and future contain the essential hopes of his soul, and he aspires to the experience of oneness outside the sensuous boundaries of life. The second goal is, of course, derived from Christian eschatalogy, but the strivings that represent it do not imply saintly beatitudes;

on the contrary, they suggest the growing secularization of Christian ideals and point to the dilemma created by such a transformation. I say dilemma because it is clear that Rousseau's efforts to achieve oneness oppose and defeat each other, for Rousseau's first search for unity presupposes a present independent of past and future, while his second search for unity depends solely on past and future, which are, without the present, only lifeless categories of the mind.

The meaning and implications of Rousseau's dilemma become clearer if one recalls the major characteristics of the eighteenth century. It is, on the one hand, dominated by neo-classicism and on the other hand, by the Enlightenment which sought to prove the self-sufficiency of intellect and nature as opposed to any transcendental or divine mediation. Ernst Cassirer and Paul Hazard have carefully analyzed the nature of these critical efforts which attempted a reappraisal of all existing values, while Becker, Frankel, Lovejoy, Mornet, Crocker, Gay and Mauzi have scrutinized the enthusiasm with which, according to Hegel, "both worlds are reconciled and heaven is transplanted to earth below."[9] There is surely as little need to review these well-known treatises as to recall the major philosophic systems of the eighteenth century, the more so, since the latter are in many ways elaborations of Lockian, Cartesian and Leibnitzian philosophies. One important fact, however, should be stressed: namely, that Descartes and his age still believed in a divine and unifying presence which guaranteed that the cleavage perceived between science and theology, mind and body, free will and a mechanical universe, was neither real nor final. The eighteenth century widened this separation, destroying at the same time any vestige of medieval oneness. There emerged two schools of thought, of which the first affirmed in a *tough-minded* manner the primacy of objective experience and knowledge, while the second school, more *tender-minded*, claimed the preeminence of subjective experience. The former implied a lack of concern with the disintegration of the substance of the self; the latter, the essential irreality of the exterior world.

Elsewhere I have attempted to show that this change was partially effected by Rousseau and Kant, the former transforming European dualism on a social, artistic, and existential level of experience.[10] Whereas the three *Critiques* forced the antinomies of the seventeenth century in a purely intellectual and moral manner, it was Rousseau's curse and greatness to expiate what Maritain chooses to call his *péché d'angélisme*—a divorce between mind and body, subjective and objective experience, instant and eternity, man and God—by *living* as well as by thinking the cleavage which he and his age had inherited. This expiation is the transmutation of Cartesian doubt (*Zweifel*) into pre-romantic despair (*Verzweiflung*). Rousseau's soul is torn. We have seen how his two attempts at finding oneness oppose each other, how one is not possible without the other, since the first search for unity presupposes a subjective present, independent of past and future, which without the present, are tragic and impossible aspirations. This tension, this shifting from one ideal to another, this estrangement in time and flight from space, represent, I believe, the true meaning of pre-romantic sensibility and also provide reasons which may account for the enthusiastic reception of Rousseau's works in France, Germany and England.

Only two decades after Rousseau's death in 1778, the sense of his contradiction had become clear to romantic philosophers and writers. They understood the schizophrenic nature of European dualism and recognized that Rousseau had lived and stated their own problems with a "fullness of heart . . . employing the whole of his being to do aught effectually."[11] On the basis of their insights into the philosophies of Spinoza, Rousseau, and Kant, the German Idealists elaborated a new myth concerning the essential oneness of life which proved to their satisfaction that the dualism from which they and their generation were suffering was nothing more than a stubborn illusion and that the totality of life's experience was in reality a harmonious *Werden* of the whole. It is fragments of this *Weltanschauung,* albeit deformed by Coleridge and Carlyle, that reached Emerson and, of course, Thoreau.

There exist, however, other bonds between Geneva and Concord. Both Rousseau and Thoreau are Protestants, Calvinists who rebelled against the tradition of an omnipotent God by making themselves the surrogate of Him. Although humorous and ironic, they are under the influence of the Protestant doctrine of the priesthood of all believers and indulge in the delivery of endless sermons to their contemporaries whom they hold in contempt, but whom they exhort to follow their example. Both men know deep guilt, for innocent men do not harangue the unseen multitude of readers, and it would be difficult to decide which of the two was more aware of his situation. In any case, their task is the same: *to save their own souls,* to be self-reformers, to be their own gods in order to forgive themselves. But as long as these rebels remain within the temporal stream of theological determinism, any pardon is illusory, for Protestant time is embedded in the eternity of God's mind; to Him, past and future are here and now; foreknowledge is an inevitable divine attribute, and predestination to ever-lasting torment or beautitude is only a finite way of expressing His understanding of human fate. It is evident that both men, yearning for complete liberation, have to enter realms outside of time, or to phrase it differently, to accede to a present which is timeless. We have shown how Rousseau reached that present in which "one is self-sufficient like God." Thoreau, possessed by the same passion for self-sufficiency on every level of experience, undertook the same journey which was facilitated by his reading of the *Bhagavat-Gita.* He seeks ". . . to stand on the meeting of two eternities, the past and future, which is precisely the present moment; to toe that line."[12] Whoever walks it is immortal: "I not yet gray on rocks forever gray, I no longer green under the evergreens. There is something even in the lapse of time by which time recovers itself."[13]

At times, the Puritan in him apologizes for the oracular nature of his remarks and screens possible guilt feelings with overt irony and good cheer: "You will pardon some abscurities, for there are more secrets in my trade than in most men's, and yet not voluntarily kept, but inseparable from its very nature. I would gladly tell all that I know about it, and never paint 'No Admittance' on my gate."[14] And since, "God himself culminates in the present moment and will never be more divine in the laps of all the ages . . ."[15] it stands to reason that the present is the gate to self-deification. Hence, ". . . we cannot afford not to live in the present. He is blessed over all mortals who loses no moment of the passing life in remembering the past,"[16]—a Puritan past laden with guilt, a past that must be denied, and I agree with Professor Lawrence Willson's suggestion that it was a Puritan impulse which sent Thoreau to seek grace in nature.[17]

These penetrations into the present, into innocence, alternate with moments of surrender to the slightest of impressions. *La cinquième rêverie du promeneur solitaire* celebrates this *dolce far niente,* and Thoreau uses similar language to describe these hours of "sheer idleness"[18] no doubt reprehensible to his fellow man. Even the settings of their rêveries are similar: they are rustic and friendly landscapes that invite herborizing and listening to the bittersweet music of a reed-pipe. Indeed, there is a great resemblance between the sober shores of the Lake of Bienne and the discreet world of Walden. But whereas Rousseau *gives* himself to these impressions "avec une sorte de volupté,"[19] Thoreau *analyzes* the impression and breaks it down to the point where his meditations become an admirable lesson in epistemology. His "intellect is a cleaver; it discerns and rifts its way into the secret of things,"[20] and in this respect it is comparable *mutatis mutandi* to the German Idealist consciousness forever bent upon invading "the inexpressible privacy of life."[21] Essentially, the American shares Rousseau's vision of beauty, and his aesthetics on motion seem to define the latter's ideal prose: "Undulation is the gentlest and most ideal of motions, produced by one fluid falling on another. Rippling is a more graceful flight. From a hilltop you may detect in it the wings of birds endlessly repeated."[22] Both authors are masters of poetic prose, Rousseau's language being more *gefühlsbeladen* or emotional, more loving and more feminine than that of Thoreau whose virile style is a rare fusion of impersonal lyricism, of romantic theology *à la* Schleiermacher and of crisp precision as practiced by English bird-watchers.

Such ecstasies of pure existence, alas, are transitory. Just as Rousseau is unable to remain still within the confines of the divine present and hence opposes to his first ideal a second ideal which in a sense is unnatural, so Thoreau forsakes Mother Nature with her "little vegetable redeemers."[23] Nature is hard to overcome, but must be overcome. He now admonishes his congregation to enter "the portals to other mansions that we occupy . . ."[24] And like the Savoyard Vicar, champion of the moral instinct, Thoreau declares that "our whole life is startlingly moral"[25] and that "he is blessed who is assured that the animal is dying out in him day by day, and the divine being established."[26] But with morality reappear the Ghosts of Past and Future, for moral deeds necessitate a temporal continuity common to all men. We have seen how Rousseau's present—the dimension of the rebellious act of self-deification—is not fused to his past and future: it cannot be. Thoreau has to face a Puritan past laden with guilt and a future heavy with chastisement. One might suggest that he, like Rousseau, challenges his brethren with moral standards so austere that their rigor precludes any possibility of fulfillment. This all too human weakness permits a curious reversal; his withdrawal from their shabby compromises is really their withdrawal from his high standards which then absolves him of non-involvement and intermittent revolutionary deeds.

These moral principles with their congruent difficulties are the basis of Rousseau's *Contrat Social*, and many propositions in the *Essay on Civil Disobedience* are reminiscent of this revolutionary document as well as of the two *Discourses* which seek to find a theoretical foundation for the political idea of Pure Right. Rousseau states the problem very clearly: "Par quel art inconcevable a-t-on pû trouver le moyen d'assujettir les hommes pour les rendre libres? d'employer au service de l'état les biens, les bras, et la vie même de tous ses membres, sans les contraindre et sans les consulter? . . . Comment se peut-il faire qu'ils obéissent et que personne ne commande, qu'ils servent et n'ayent point de maître . . . Ces prodiges sont l'ouvrage de la loi. . . . C'est cette voix céleste qui dicte à chaque citoyen les préceptes de la raison publique, et lui apprend à agir selon les maximes de son propre jugement, et à n'être pas en contradiction avec lui-même (III, 248). Rousseau's notion of *la volonté générale* is derived from this important concept of the *Law*. Thoreau admits its existence:" . . . a corporation of conscientious men is a corporation *with* a conscience,"[27] but he refuses to make such a corporation the end and purpose of his ideal society which is anarchistic: " 'That government is best which governs not at all'; and when men are prepared for it, that will be the kind of government which they will have. Government is at best an expedient."[28] Given the simplistic nature of some of Thoreau's concepts concerning society, one may safely assume that he was not acquainted with the profound sociological analyses of Rousseau and Kant. Furthermore, his *a priori* rejection of political solutions may well have been intensified by the political failure of the French Revolution, the specific milieu of the extreme Abolitionists as well as his personal situation.

There exist, to be sure, other concordances between the two thinkers. Both, fearful and contemptuous of possession in every sense of the word, oppose at various times the identification of property and freedom in the manner of Locke and Montesquieu and in so doing deny their Calvinist capitalist tradition which had always fused the concepts and experiences of property and political freedom. They are not only rebels, but also true revolutionaries who question the whole system, indeed civilization itself. The style of their attack is identical. With angry logic they confront the sorry realities of "dirty institutions"[29] with the shiny *mystique* of their dreams; and by a cunning and consistent use of paradox and epigram, they lay bare and condemn the real and apparent inconsistencies of the others, while granting themselves the privilege of pure motives and prophetic utterance. In short, they tyrannize their tyrants. Their critiques differ however, for Thoreau is more polemical and openly destructive. He resists actively and passively, while Rousseau, more theoretical, seeks to fill the void within him and around him by proposing utopian systems: the *Emile* prescribing the education of the new man, *La Nouvelle Héloïse* the ideals of the new family, and *Le Contrat Social* the structure of the new republic.[30]

Whether Rousseau's and Thoreau's mediations of individualistic and social experience are brilliant compromises or admirable reconciliations is, in the final analysis, as unknowable as the question of their respective defeats and victories in their quest *to be* and *to be aware of being*. What is certain is that Rousseau and Thoreau committed themselves to the discovery of "the essential facts of life," and that in so doing they delineated in a clear and painful light a perennial dilemma of the human mind. Quixotic, they sought to combine life and poetry, discovering to their sorrow that, on the ultimate level, thought and being appear to exclude each other and that the final unity that man yearns for be it the mystic union with God, be it a lasting union with the beloved woman,[31] or be it a union with oneself, remains a tragically unattainable ideal.

It could be shown that this latter quest is also a specific characteristic of the romantic soul, and Fichte's *Bestimmung des Menschen* or *Vocation of Man* and Hegel's *Phenomenology of Mind* are genial illustrations of this curse. The desire for unity is *la passion maîtresse* of the Romantics. Kant achieves it on the intellectual and moral level (the synthetic unity of apperception), but is forced, by the nature of his system, to leave out the existential component of men's experience, whereas Rousseau, artist and existentialist, could never forego living at the crossroads of the spiritual and sensuous worlds, whose conscious and involuntary recollection became the very source of his genius. He had suffered too much to limit the absolute reality of his self and attempted in vain to integrate and balance all factors of the human equation. His identity, we have seen, is hopelessly split, and the *poetic* truth he does experience is always in the past, for to write about one's life is to reflect on what has been and the happiness which he, like

Thoreau, swears to have known, becomes but a dream: "Hélas, mon plus constant bonheur fut en songe" (I, 108). Their evocations of the pure present, be it that of the *Ile de Saint-Pierre* or of Walden Pond are always engendered in its shadow, and imply a genetic falsification which even the *écriture automatique* of the Surrealists could not avoid.

Thoreau was aware of this rift: "My life has been the poem I would have writ, / But I could not both live and utter it,"[32] or elsewhere: "Each melodious note I hear / Brings this reproach to me / That I alone afford the ear / Who would the music be."[33] Being a full-fledged Romantic as well as one of Kant's epigones, he understands and suffers the dilemma that Rousseau lived: "I only know myself as a human entity; the scene, so to speak, of thoughts and affections; and am sensible of a certain doubleness by which I can stand as remote from myself as from another. However intense my experience, I am conscious of the presence and criticism of a part of me, which, as it were, is not a part of me, but spectator, sharing no experience, but taking note of it; and that is no more I than it is you. When the play, it may be the tragedy, of life is over, the spectator goes his way. It was a kind of fiction, a work of the imagination only . . ."[34] These lines could have been written by Valéry, for they stress the modernity of Thoreau, who conceived himself, like so many contemporary minds, as a logical identity, timeless and detached from fleeting affections, and yet continuously menaced by disintegration and saddened by the unattainability of peace and unity.[35]

104 Essays on Rousseau

Footnotes to Chapter I

Unless indicated otherwise, all references to Rousseau's *Confessions* and to his *Rêveries du promeneur solitaire* relate to the édition Pléiade (*Oeuvres complètes*, 4 vol., 1959–1969). Roman numerals refer to vol.

1. L. F. Benedetto, *Mme de Warens* (Paris, 1914), pp. 26, 7. Concerning the relationship between Rousseau and Mme de Warens, see François Mugnier, *Mme de Warens et J. J. Rousseau* (Paris, 1891); Hélène Pittard, "J. J. Rousseau et Mme de Warens," *Revue des deux mondes* (Oct. 1, 1924); A. Schinz, *Etat présent des travaux sur J. J. Rousseau* (Paris and New York, 1941).

2. Concerning the question of Rousseau's sincerity, consult Henri Peyre, *Literature and Sincerity* (New Haven, 1963), chapt. 3: "We believe that Rousseau reached a degree of good faith to himself unequaled in his time and not often if ever equaled by the romantics who were his progeny, in France, in Germany, in England, or by the great Russian, Tolstoi, who worshipped him, literally, as his saint. A Danish philosopher, Harald Höffding, who wrote one of the best studies on Rousseau's thought and was also an expert in psychology, declared: 'If Rousseau had not given us his *Confessions* we should lack one of the most important contributions to the knowledge of human nature.' " *Op. cit.*, p. 107.

3. Jean Guéhenno, *Jean-Jacques—En marge des Confessions* (Paris, 1948), I, p. 10.

4. The problem of time in the *Confessions* has been studied by Georges Poulet and Georges Gusdorf. The former's book, *Etudes sur le temps humain* (Paris, 1950) has an excellent chapter on Rousseau's experience of time, while the latter's treatise, *Mémoire et Personne*, 2 vols. (Paris, 1950) contains an interesting paragraph on Rousseau's memory. These two critics, however, hardly concern themselves with the time of the artist, that is, illusory or artificial duration. See also Mark Temmer, *Time in Rousseau and Kant* (Geneva, 1958). Consult also an informative article by Lionel Gossman "Time and History in Rousseau" in *Studies on Voltaire and the Eighteenth Century*, 1964, XXX, pp. 311–349.

5. *Oeuvres complètes*, ed. V. D. Musset-Pathay, XIII (1823–26), 50, 1.

6. *Op. cit.*, p. 111.

7. Goethe's evocation of Wilhelm Meister on the march suggests an obvious kinship to Jean-Jacques' daydreams about his journey to Chambéry:

Die Witterung war schön, und jedermann stimmte leicht in den Vorschlag ein. Wilhelm eilte zu Fuss durch das Gebirge voraus, und über seine sonderbare Gestalt musste jeder, der ihm begegnete, stutzig werden. Er eilte mit schnellen und zufriedenen Schritten den Wald hinauf, Laertes pfiff hinter ihm drein, nur die Frauen liessen sich in den Wagen fortschleppen. Mignon lief gleichfalls nebenher, stolz auf den Hirschfänger, den man ihr, als die Gesellschaft sich bewaffnete, nicht abschlagen konnte. Um ihren Hut hatte sie die Perlenschnur gewunden, die Wilhelm von Marianens Reliquien übrigbehalten hatte. Friedrich der Blonde trug die Flinte des Laertes, der Harfner hatte das friedlichste Ansehen. Sein langes Kleid war in den Gürtel gesteckt, und so ging er freier. Er stützte sich auf einen knotigen Stab, sein Instrument war bei den Wagen zurückgeblieben.
Nachdem sie nicht ganz ohne Beschwerlichkeit die Höhe erstiegen, erkannten sie sogleich den angezeigten Platz an den schönen Buchen, die ihn umgaben und bedeckten. Eine grosse, sanft abhängige Waldwiese lud zum Bleiben ein; eine eingefasste Quelle bot die lieblichste Erquickung dar, und es zeigte sich an der andern Seite durch Schluchten und Waldrücken eine ferne, schöne und hoffnungsvolle Aussicht. Da lagen Dörfer und Mühlen in den Gründen,

Städtchen in der Ebene, und neue, in der Ferne eintretende Berge machten die Aussicht noch hoffnungsvoller, indem sie nur wie eine sanfte Beschränkung hereintraten.

Wilhelm Meisters Lehrjahre, ed. Trunz, Hamburger Ausgabe, VII, p. 222. Eichendorff's treatment of the same theme is even closer to the Rousseauean model:

Als ich eine Strecke so fort gewandert war, sah ich rechts von der Strasse einen sehr schönen Baumgarten, wo die Morgensonne so lustig zwischen den Stämmen und Wipfeln hindurchschimmerte, dass es aussah, als wäre der Rasen mit goldenen Teppichen belegt. Da ich keinen Menschen erblickte, stieg ich über den niedrigen Gartenzaun und legte mich recht behaglich unter einem Apfelbaum ins Gras, denn von dem gestrigen Nachtlager auf dem Baume taten mir noch alle Glieder weh. Da konnte man weit ins Land hinaussehen, und da es Sonntag war, so kamen bis aus der weitesten Ferne Glockenklänge über die stillen Felder herüber, und geputzte Landleute zogen überall zwischen Wiesen und Büschen nach der Kirche. Ich war recht fröhlich im Herzen, die Vögel sangen über mir im Baume, ich dachte an meine Mühle und an den Garten der schönen gnädigen Frau, und wie das alles nun so weit, weit lag . . .

Eichendorff, *Werke,* II, *Aus dem Leben eines Taugenichts* (Stuttgart, 1957), p. 370.

8. Concerning Mme de Warens' legacy of letters written to her by Rousseau, cf. R. A. Leigh, "Jean-Jacques Rousseau and Madame de Warens—Some recently discovered documents" in *Studies on Voltaire and the Eighteenth Century,* 1969, LXVII, pp. 165–175.

9. From the viewpoint of the literary history of the West, Rousseau's unforgettable portrait of Mme de Warens represents perhaps the first in-depth biography of the emotions, attitudes, and actions of a woman from her youth until her death. Maman lived, and Jean-Jacques made her come alive. Greek biography does not offer fully drawn portraits of women, and the portraits of women Greek authors do draw are usually an integral part of epic, dramatic, or narrative movements, as for instance, in the *Iliad,* where Homer grants us glimpses of Helen through the eyes of the elders. Indeed, even within a strictly fictional context, the Greek heroines that are most developed, as for example, Penelope, Euripides' Andromache or Apollonios' Medea, appear quite far removed from the ambiguous, fleeting and sometimes hard facts of *l'existence vécue* so dear to contemporary authors like Joyce and Moravia.

Similarly, the Roman literary heroines like Dido, Lesbia, or Cynthia are not envisaged as palpable and aging creatures, in that they are essentially artistic creations unscathed by time, while, as I have tried to show, Rousseau's evocation of Mme de Warens represents a biographical artistic portrait throbbing with the pulse of time. Jean-Jacques' favorite author, Plutarch, is, in truth, the first biographer of women, his most celebrated evocations being those of Cleopatra, Fulvia, and Octavia. Yet, however splendidly depicted, the Queen of Egypt does not develop in a modern psychological sense, but rather is seen only in action. Likewise, Tacitus' portrait of Agrippina, despite his innuendoes, creates an illusion of objective reality without ever probing the drives and motives of the character. Byzantine chroniclers (Procopius, Psellus) are no more analytical than either Tacitus or Plutarch—their relations and anecdotes concerning the lives of Theodora, Zoe and other empresses consisting in the main of sundry political and amorous intrigues.

The Bible and Christian hagiographers are even less explicit in matters pertaining to the existential biography of women than Roman and Byzantine historians and biographers, their respective saints and sinners lacking an identity in the modern sense of the word. Ruth, Naomi, and Esther, for instance, exemplify above all pastoral, ethical, and political ideas and attitudes. The reasons for this state of affairs appear to be threefold: first, the paternalistic structure of the Greco-Roman and Judeo-Christian world precluded any ontological emphasis on woman as a creature equal to man; second, the idea of character, development, or *Bildung*, was a notion essentially alien to the classical world (cf. our discussion of this problem in the chapter comparing Goethe's *Bildungsroman* to Rousseau's *Nouvelle Héloïse*); third, in the words of Wilamowitz: ". . . just as the Hellenes produced no real historical works, they were unable to conceive an individual man in the full reality of his existence . . .",[1] that is to say, human *existence* in the Heideggerian sense of the word was to the Greek mind nothing but a raw material which attained a status worth mentioning only after it had been refined in the crucibles of will, courage, art, and intellect. Although more feminist in its outlook than classical and biblical traditions, medieval literature (the troubadours, Chrétien de Troyes, Dante) restricts its evocation of women in its fiction and its historical writing according to fairly rigid mytho-poetic, religious, and social codes which serve as points of departure for poetic and spiritual analyses[2]—the great exception to the rule being the portrait of Héloïse as it emerges from the *Letters*. Her character throbs with life and foreshadows the anonymous author of the *Letters of a Portugese Nun* as well as Julie, *la prêcheuse*, embodiment of all the women Rousseau ever knew and dreamt of. Other exceptions transcending in varying degrees the stereotypical patterns of medieval fiction are Fénice, Iseut (Thomas and Gottfried von Strassburg) and Jean de Meung's *vieille* in *Le Roman de la Rose*, and one has to wait for Chaucer's Wife of Bath rather than his Cressida to encounter in fiction the first true ancestor of Mme de Warens. Memorable by virtue of her strength grounded in life, Alisoun imposes her presence with primordial force. She loves like a woman and thinks like a man and, above all, brushes aside any stereotypical limitation of her being to achieve a powerful affirmation of her unique identity and the justice of her desires:

> Men may conseille a womman to been oon,
> But conseilling is no comandement . . .

Indeed, despite the fact that the Wife of Bath is a literary creation, she embodies extraordinary resemblances to Madame de Warens; both women enjoy *le plaisir d'être* so dear to the hearts of Chaucer and Rousseau, both women are free women and to some extent polygamous, a fact whose importance cannot be overestimated given that the traditionally paternalistic *Weltanschauung* of Western culture has always impeded the development and emancipation of women and perhaps in the final analysis that of men.

1. "Die Autobiographie im Altertum," *Internat. Wochenschrift für Wissenschaft* (1907, I, pp. 1105 sqq.) quoted by Georg Misch, *A History of Autobiography in Antiquity* (London, 1950), preface to the 2nd edition, p. x.

2. "Quoi qu'on en ait dit," asserts Paul Zumthor, "la poésie courtoise restait un monde verbal, et ne rencontrait que par hasard la vie." *Lettres de Héloïse et Abélard* (Lausanne, 1950), postface, p. 178.

Footnotes to Chapter II

Unless indicated otherwise, all quotations from Rousseau refer to his *Oeuvres complètes,* 4 vol. éd. Pléiade (1959–1969). Whenever possible, footnotes are incorporated in the text. Roman numerals refer to volumes.

1. du Bellay, *La Deffence et l'Illustration de la Langue Francoyse,* éd. Em. Person (Paris, 1892), p. 117.

2. Mia Gerhardt, *La pastorale—essai d'analyse littéraire* (Assen, 1950), p. 290.

3. Tasso, *Aminta, Opere* I, ed. Bruno Maier (Milano, 1963), I, Sc. 1, 11. 231–3, p. 100.

4. Bernardin de Saint-Pierre, *Oeuvres complètes* (Paris, 1826), VIII, p. 280.

5. To the best of my knowledge, Francis Gribble was the first to refer to *l'Idylle des Cerises* as being a pastoral idyll. In his hostile commentary, he devotes one sentence to it: "The incident as described by him is quite a pastoral idyll, but it has no importance. Nothing came of it either at the time or afterwards . . ." *Rousseau and the Women He Loved* (New York, 1908), p. 68.

6. On the relatively small contribution of the Christian pastoral ideal to the pastoral genre, consult W. W. Greg, *Pastoral Poetry and Pastoral Drama* (London, 1906), p. 21 ff. Also consult Renato Poggioli, "Naboth's Vineyard or the Pastoral View of the Social Order," *JHI*, XXIV, 1963; "Dante Poco Tempo Silvano: Or a 'Pastoral Oasis' in the Commedia," *80th Annual Report of the Dante Society*, 1962; and "The Oaten Flute," *Harvard Library Bulletin*, XI, 1957. Concerning Rousseau's *Le lévite d'Ephraïm,* see footnote 8. Another general treatment of the pastoral is by Thomas Rosenmeyer, *The Green Cabinet* (Berkeley, 1969). For a very thorough reference work, consult, Renate Böschenstein, *Idylle* (Stuttgart, 1967).

7. Consult the *Confessions* where Rousseau describes his visit to the landscape of *l'Astrée* as well as his analysis of his *état d'âme* preceding his love affair with Mme d'Houdetot: "J'allai malheureusement me rappeler le diné du Château de Toun et ma rencontre avec ces deux charmantes filles dans la même saison et dans des lieux à peu près semblables à ceux où j'étois en ce moment . . . Mon sang s'allume et petille, la tête me tourne malgré mes cheveux déja grisonnans, et voila le grave Citoyen de Genève, voila l'austére Jean Jaques à près de quarante cinq ans redevenu tout à coup le berger extravagant" (I, 426, 7). Throughout his writings, Rousseau stresses his love for pastoral ideals and novels, and Seillière and Faguet only amplify Rousseau's succinct statement concerning his mother's bequest: "Ma mere avoit laissé des Romans" (I, 8). A propos, Starobinski declares: ". . . ces romans [ceux de Rousseau] sont un vestige de la mère perdue," *Jean-Jacques Rousseau La transparence et l'obstacle* (Paris, 1957), p. 6.

8. Renato Poggioli, "The Pastoral of the Self," *Daedalus*, Fall, 1959, p. 887: "One should, however, never forget that the ultimate representative of the pastoral self was bound to be another and less fictitious Jacques [the other being Shakespeare's Jaques]—the greatest literary figure of the eighteenth century, Jean-Jacques Rousseau . . ." In his article "The Oaten Flute" Poggioli asserts: ". . . that the pastoral longing is but the wishful dream of a happiness to be gained without effort, of an erotic bliss made absolute by its own irresponsibility. This, rather than a sense of decency, is the very reason why the pastoral often limits the sexual embrace to mere kissing, so as to escape the danger of parenthood, and the nuisance of birth control. (In this connection, nothing is more typical in a pastoral sense than the episode of Rousseau's *Confessions* that goes under the name of *l'Idylle des Cerises*") p. 159. With due respect to Poggioli, I think that he missed the point completely. Unfortunately, Rosenmeyer subscribes to this simplification. Daniel Mornet dwells at length on Rousseau's fondness for idylls and comments on his attempt to emulate

Gessner by writing a biblical idyll *Le lévite d'Ephraïm*. He concludes his *Sentiment de la Nature en France:* "Rousseau parle en son nom, non sous les déguisements des bergers d'idylle et du ton compassé des "poètes descriptifs . . ." p. 463. However, it seems to me that Mornet disregards Rousseau's originality in creating the modern idyll as defined by Schiller and Jean-Paul.

9. Jules Marsan, *La pastorale dramatique française* (Paris, 1905), p. 452.

10. Rousseau, *Corresp. gén.,* éd. T. Dufour (Paris, 1925), III, p. 13, lettre à Tronchin, 17 janvier, 1757. Concerning Rousseau's knowledge of Latin authors, specifically Virgil, see *Confessions* (I, 238, 9).

11. Did Longus influence Rousseau's conception of *l'Idylle des Cerises?* There exist undeniable analogies to which we refer below. Bernardin de Saint-Pierre relates that "J. J. Rousseau avait également composé la musique de Daphnis et Chloe . . ." in *Fragments sur J. J. Rousseau, op. cit.,* XII, p. 31.

12. On the relationship between Rousseau and Italian authors, we have on hand several studies of which L. F. Benedetto's essay is most pertinent to our subject-matter. His analysis deals mainly with Rousseau's interpretation of Tasso's personality and the influence of *La Gerusalemme liberata* on *La Nouvelle Héloïse.* Especially important to our argument are the following comments: ". . . il Rousseau ha talvolta la pena voluttuosa come il Tasso, il suo poeta favorito, ma si può ravvisare nella sua forma più realistica la torbida attività in cui il poeta italiano metteva la sua fantasia lussuriosa," "Jean-Jacques Rousseau Tassofiglio" in *Scritti varii di erudizione e di critica in onore di Rodolfo Renier* (Torino, 1912), p. 373. Also interesting is Benedetto's remark that "L'autore del *Devin du Village* aprì certo la sua anima con compiacimento infinito al lacrimoso sorriso di voluttà che splende nell'incomparabile *Aminta* . . ." p. 374. Chandler B. Beall summarizes Benedetto's arguments and situates Rousseau's predilection within the larger context of his study *La Fortune du Tasse en France* (Eugene, 1942), chapt. x. To be consulted lightheartedly is Carlo Culcasi's *Gli influssi italiani nell'opera di G. G. Rousseau* (Roma, 1907). In this somewhat unscholarly investigation, one finds repeated affirmations rather based on flair than on proof (I suspect Culcasi may have been right) that *l'Aminta* has played a decisive role in the shaping of Rousseau's literary imagination: "Il Tasso è il poeta la cui utopia è più affine a quella del Rousseau, e *l'Aminta* è l'opera che mostra più visibili quelle tendenze che svolse e sviluppò il ginevrino," *op. cit.,* p. 105. Furthermore, he bases his airy arguments on a book by Charlotte Banti, *l'Amyntas et l'Astrée* (Milan, 1895). Benedetto limits the influence of *l'Aminta* to two passages in *La Nouvelle Héloïse, op. cit.,* p. 374.

13. Concerning the historical background of *l'Idylle* consult François et Joseph Serand, *Un épisode de la vie de J. J. Rousseau—l'Idylle des Cerises* (Chambéry, 1928). Arsène Houssaye believes that Rousseau's inspiration came from a gouache by Baudouin, Boucher's son-in-law. It was exhibited in 1760 and bears the title "Les cerises et les amoureuses." Houssaye asserts that it is "un petit chef-d'œuvre d'esprit et de volupté. Or, c'est mot à mot celui de Rousseau. Voyez plutôt la gravure qui est partout: ces deux belles filles qui attendent les cerises, gorge entr'ouverte et bras demi-nus, ne sont-ce pas les visions de Jean-Jacques? Et ce galant qui cueille les cerises et qui les jette avec intention, n'est-ce pas Jean-Jacques lui-même? C'est-à-dire que Jean-Jacques, au lieu de se souvenir d'une page de sa vie, s'est souvenu d'un tableau de Baudouin. A moins qu'il n'ait conté son histoire au peintre; mais alors n'eut-il pas dit cela, en écrivant les *Confessions.*" *Les Charmettes— J. J. Rousseau et Madame de Warens* (Paris, 1863), p. 45.

14. J. G. Frazer, *The Golden Bough* (New York), 1956, abridged ed. p. 371.

15. Roscher, *Ausführliches Lexikon der Griechischen und Römischen Mythologie* (Leipzig, 1884–1886), I, p. 962.

16. *Aminta*, II, Sc. 1, 1. 780, p. 131.

17. Hölderlin, "Rousseau," *Sämtliche Gedichte* (Berlin, 1942), pp. 244–5, quoted by Starobinski, *op. cit.*, p. 16.

18. *Op. cit.*, p. 301.

19. A similar *idylle à trois* will be that of Saint-Preux and his "deux charmantes amies."

20. On this point, it is worthwhile to quote Karl Vossler: "Es ist sehr bezeichnend, dass die Pastourelle auf italienischem Boden nicht recht gedeihen wollte. Es fehlte die gesellschaftliche Voraussetzung: der Gegensatz zwischen Feudalität und Bauernstand. Italien war ein demokratisches Land—und als der hochtrabende Ritterepos über die Alpen herabstieg da ging es auch mit seiner Würde, je tiefer es ins Land kam, abwärts." "Tassos *Aminta* und die *Hirtendichtung*," *Studien zur vergleichenden Literaturgeschichte*, Berlin, 1906, vol. VI, pp. 28, 9.

21. *Aminta*, II, 11. 765–7, p. 131.

22. *Op. cit.*, p. 169.

23. The epigraph of this chapter constitutes the prologue. Act I ends with the passage: ". . . mais l'absente revenoit bien vite . . ." Act II consists of the next two paragraphs which conclude with "pour la sensualité." The third act is limited to the delightful scene of the cherry tree. The ensuing paragraph contains the fourth act. The fifth act begins with "Enfin elles se souvinrent qu'il ne falloit pas attendre la nuit . . ." and ends with "nous trouvames que nous avions eu le secret de la [journée] faire longue par tous les amusemens dont nous avions su la remplir." The epilogue begins with "Je les quittai à peu près au même endroit où elles m'avoient pris . . ." and ends with: "nos éphémeres amours?"

24. Theocritus, *Idyll* VII, ed. and transl. A. S. F. Gow (Cambridge, 1952), I, p. 65. For a very fine translation of Theocritus, see: Horst Rüdiger, *Griechische Lyriker* (Zürich, 1949).

25. Ernst Robert Curtius, *European Literature and the Latin Middle Ages* (New York, 1953), p. 191 ff.

26. For a summary of problems pertaining to the etymological and historical development of the words *idylle and églogue* consult Alice Hulubei, *L'églogue en France au XVe siècle* (Paris, 1938), pp. xi–xiii. For a more recent summary of the same problem, consult also: Renate Böschenstein, *op. cit.*, pp. 2–5.

27. *Aminta*, ed. A. Tortoretto (Milano, 1946), p. 12.

28. *Ibid.*, Act II, Sc. 3, 1. 1067, p. 148.

29. Milton, *Comus*, in *Complete Poems and Major Prose*, ed. Hughes (New York, 1957), 11. 122–6, p. 93. Cf. also: "L'innocente joye aime à s'évaporer au grand jour, mais le vice est l'ami des ténebres, et jamais l'innocence et le mistere n'abiteret longtems ensemble." *La Nouvelle Héloïse*, 4th part, 10th letter, p. 457.

30. *Op. cit.*, p. 37.

31. Mario Praz, "Milton and Poussin," in *Seventeenth Century Studies Presented to Sir Herbert Grierson* (Oxford, 1938), p. 202.

32. Vladimir Jankélévitch, *Le pur et l'impur* (Paris, 1960), p. 7, 14.

33. Consult Starobinski's analysis of Rousseau's value system: "La norme n'est plus transcendante, elle est immanente au moi," *op. cit.*, p. 21; also "L'imitation de Jésus-Christ, chez Rousseau, est l'imitation de l'acte 'divin' par lequel une conscience humaine devient source de vérité . . ." *Ibid.*, p. 25. On the question of self-deification, see M. Temmer, *Time in Rousseau and Kant* (Geneva, 1958), chapt. I.

34. Starobinski's commentary on Rousseau's *Morceau allégorique* relates to my viewpoint: "Le dieu-homme (comme d'ailleurs Rousseau lui-même) s'offre à tous les regards non pour être vu lui-même, mais pour qu'une source sacrée soit reconnue dans l'acte même par lequel il parle et se communique sans restriction," *op. cit.*, p. 83.

35. Cf. Panofsky's essay "Et in Arcadia Ego," in *The Meaning in the Visual*

Arts (New York, 1955): "In Virgil's ideal Arcady human suffering and super-humanly perfect surroundings create a dissonance. This dissonance, once felt, had to be resolved, and it was resolved in that vespertinal mixture of sadness and tranquillity which is perhaps Virgil's most personal contribution to poetry." p. 300.

36. René Rapin, *De Carmine Pastorali*, prefixed to Thomas Creech's translation of the *Idylliums* of Theocritus (1684), Ann Arbor, The Augustan Reprint Society, 1947), p. 26, p. 56.

37. Fontenelle, *Discours sur la nature de l'églogue*, *Oeuvres* (Paris, 1825), V, p. 42.

38. *Ibid.*

39. Samuel Johnson, *The Rambler*, quoted by Greg, *op. cit.*, p. 416.

40. *Op. cit.*, p. 2.

41. J. H. Herder, *Sämtliche Werke*, ed. Suphan (Berlin, 1887), vol. I, p. 338: "Was ist nunmehr die Idylle? Nichts als der sinnlichste Ausdruck der höchst verschönerten Leidenschaften und Empfindungen solcher Menschen, die in kleinern Gesellschaften zusammen leben."

42. Cf. William Empson, *Some Versions of Pastoral* (Norfolk, 1950).

43. Schiller, *Complete Works*, 8 vol. (New York, 1902) *On Simple and Sentimental Poetry*, VIII, p. 305.

44. *Ibid.*, p. 306.

45. *Ibid.*

46. *Ibid.*, p. 320.

47. *Ibid.*, p. 324.

48. Horst Rüdiger, "Schiller und das Pastorale" in *Euphorion*, vol. 53, 1959, p. 240.

49. Cf. Karl Mannheim, "Das utopische Bewusstsein" in *Ideologie und Utopie* (Bonn, 1930).

50. Jean Paul Richter, *Sämtliche Werke—Vorschule der Aesthetik* (Weimar, 1935), XI, paragraph 73, "Die Idylle," pp. 241–4.

51. *Ibid.*

52. Concerning the influence of Gessner, see Paul Van Tieghem, "Les Idylles de Gessner et le Rêve pastoral dans le Préromantisme Européen," *Revue de Littérature Comparée*, 1942, pp. 41–72, 222–69: "On sent confusément que le genre pastoral porte en lui des possibilités presque infinies de développements," p. 46. Van Tieghem also comments at length on Rousseau's reaction on reading Huber's translation of Gessner's *Idylle* which Usteri had brought to his attention: "Ah! c'est un auteur charmant que M. Gessner. Je voudrais qu'il écrivît toutes les années trois cent soixante-cinq idylles et que je pusse en lire tous les jours une nouvelle." Quoted from *Corresp. de J. J. Rousseau avec Leonard Usteri*, éd. Usteri and Ritter (Zürich and Geneva, 1910), lettre du 6 juin, 1764.

53. Cf. Montaigne: "Quand je dance, je dance; quand je dors, je dors; voyre et quand je me promeine solitairement en un beau vergier, si mes pensées se sont entretenues des occurrences estrangieres quelque partie du temps, quelque autre partie je les rameine à la promenade, au vergier, à la douceur de cette solitude et à moy." *Essais*, "De l'expérience" (éd. Pléiade, 1946), p. 1079.

54. *Op. cit.* VI, p. 84.

55. *Jocelyn*, éd. Jean des Cognets (Paris, 1960), p. 118.

56. Enrico Carrara, *La Poesia Pastorale* (Milano, 1904–8), p. 474.

57. George Sand, *François le Champi* (Paris, 1888), pp. 16, 7. Proustians, remembering *Maman's* careful expurgation of all love passages in *François le Champi* when reading it to little Marcel, may find George Sand's preface to her novel *Les Maîtres Mosaïstes* quite amusing: "J'ai écrit les *Mosaïstes* en 1847, pour mon fils, qui n'avait encore lu qu'un roman, *Paul et Virginie*. Cette

lecture était trop forte pour les nerfs d'un pauvre enfant. Il avait tant pleuré, que je lui avais promis de lui faire un roman où il n'y aurait pas d'amour et où toutes choses finiraient pour le mieux . . ." p. 10.

58. Balzac, *Le lys dans la vallée* (Vienne, Manz éd.), p. 30.

59. Proust, *A la recherche du temps perdu* (éd. Pléiade, 1954), I, pp. 797, 8.

60. Camus, *L'homme révolté* (Paris, 1951), pp. 171, 2.

61. Camus, *Noces* (Paris, 1950), p. 30.

62. Renato Poggioli, "Naboth's Vineyard or the Pastoral View," *op. cit.*, p. 24.

63. Goethe, *Herman und Dorothea, Werke* (Leipzig) ed. Alt, vol. XV, 11. 273, 4, p. 172.

64. Horst Rüdiger, "Weltliteratur in Goethes 'Helena' " in *Jahrbuch der deutschen Schillergesellschaft* (Stuttgart, 1964), p. 193.

65. Kleist, *Sämtliche Werke*, ed. Zweig, (München, 1923) IV, letter to Ulrike, May 1, 1802, pp. 424, 5. Consult Roger Ayrault, *Heinrich von Kleist*, Paris, Nizet et Bastard, 1934 (Thèse de Sorbonne). pp. 286–304.

66. *Op. cit.*, p. 86.

67. Thomas Mann, *Der Zauberberg* (Berlin, 1926), p. 648.

68. Georg Crabbe, "The Village," *Poetical Works* (London, 1861), Bk I, p. 114.

69. Jacques Voisine, *J. J. Rousseau en Angleterre à l'époque romantique* (Paris, 1956). For a perceptive analysis of the influence of Rousseau's 5e *promenade* on Shelley's *Alastor*, consult, Donald L. Maddox, "Shelley's *Alastor* and the Legacy of Rousseau" in *Studies in Romanticism*, IX, Spring 1970, Number 2, pp. 82–98.

70. Hazlitt, *Complete Works*, ed. Howe, (London, 1930), IV, p. 92.

71. George Meredith, *The Ordeal of Richard Feverel* (London, 1914), p. 118.

72. Guillén, *Cánticos* "Mas allá" (Mexico, 1945), p. 18.

73. Henri Peyre, *Bibliographie critique de l'hellénisme en France de 1843–1870* (New Haven, 1932).

74. Henri Peyre, *L'influence des littératures antiques sur la littérature française moderne* (New Haven, 1941), p. 3.

75. Cf. Robert Mauzi, *L'idée du bonheur au XVIIIe siècle* (Paris, 1965). Consult also a witty and informative article by the late Helmuth Petriconi, "Die verlorenen Paradiese," in *Romanistisches Jahrbuch*, vol. X, 1959, pp. 167–199.

Footnotes to Chapter III

Unless indicated otherwise, all references to Goethe's *Werke* relate to the *Hamburger Ausgabe*, ed. by Trunz, XIV vol., (Hamburg, 1965). Roman numerals refer to volumes. All references to Rousseau relate to the édition Pléiade, *Oeuvres complètes*, 4 vol., (1959–1969). Whenever possible, references to Goethe and Rousseau have been integrated into the text.

1. Merker und Stammler, *Reallexikon der deutschen Literaturgeschichte*, (Berlin, 1950) I, p. 175. Karl Viëtor expounds a similar view: "Auch die anderen Nationen haben solche Entwicklungs- oder Bildungsromane; aber unter den Deutschen allein ist der Bildungsroman zu solcher Blüte und Vollendung gelangt, dass man ihn geradezu *die* deutsche Spezies des modernen Romans nennen und darin ein gewichtiges Argument für die Ansicht sehen darf, die modernen Deutschen seien in höherem Masse als die andern europäischen Nationen ein individualistisches Volk." *Goethe* (Bern, 1949), p. 133.

2. Erich Schmidt, *Richardson, Rousseau* und *Goethe*, (Jena, 1875), p. 130.

3. *Ibid.*, p. 131.

4. Max Wundt, *Goethes Wilhelm Meister und die Entwicklung des modernen Lebensideals*, (Berlin, 1913), p. 52.

5. Wilhelm Dilthey, *Das Leben Schleiermachers*, 2nd ed. vol. I, 1922, p. 317. Fritz Martini notes that the term "Bildungsroman" was not coined by Dilthey, but that it first appeared in two lectures by Karl von Morgenstern in 1819, his models being *Agathon* and *Wilhelm Meister*, "Der Bildungsroman—Zur Geschichte des Wortes und der Theorie" *Dvjs*, 35, 1961, pp. 44–63. Martini comments: "Der von Morgenstern eilig mit ungeschickten Namenshäufungen vollgezogene Gang durch die europäische Romangeschichte lässt unklar, ob mit den genannten Werken jeweils von ihm der Bildungsroman gemeint sei. Er vermisst ihn bei den Italienern, er nennt den 'Don Quixote' das erste klassische Muster des neuern Romans, er hebt den 'Télémaque' von Fénelon als einen in seiner Art sehr schätzbaren Bildungsroman von beschränktem Zweck in der französischen Romanliteratur hervor, ebenso den pädagogischen Bildungsroman 'Emile' von Rousseau." *Ibid.*, p. 61.

6. Wilhelm Dilthey, *Das Erlebnis und die Dichtung*, 8th ed. (Leipzig, 1922), pp. 393, 4.

7. *Ibid.*, p. 217.

8. Melitta Gerhard, *Der deutsche Entwicklungsroman bis zu Goethes 'Wilhelm Meister'* (Halle, 1926), p. 90.

9. *Ibid.*, p. 151.

10. *Ibid.*, p. 123.

11. Hans Heinrich Borcherdt, *Der Roman der Goethezeit* (Stuttgart, 1949), p. 14.

12. *Ibid.*, p. 10.

13. E. Buss, "Rousseau und die deutsche Literatur," in *Allgemeine Deutsche Lehrerszeitung*, 1912, p. 310.

14. Edmond Vermeil, "Goethe et Rousseau," *Annales de la Société J.-J. Rousseau*, 1946–49, vol. XXXI, p. 65. In the same article, Vermeil considers Rousseau's novel as the mother-cell of the major literary works by Goethe: "En ce qui concerne la production romanesque de Goethe, la démonstration n'est pas des plus difficiles. Notons tout d'abord qu'au roman de Rousseau, surtout à la deuxième partie et à ses considérations sur le mariage, puis aux *Confessions* correspondent, du côté de Goethe, *La vocation dramatique de W. Meister*, ses *Années d'apprentissage*, ses *Années de voyage*, les *Affinités électives*, enfin les *Mémoires* et les autres écrits autobiographiques de Goethe. De ce point de vue, Werther m'apparaît comme un Saint-Preux qui se tue parce qu'il est, lui aussi, fatalement séparé de celle qu'il aime et que les préjugés sociaux compromettent également sa carrière. Mais l'évolution de W. Meister, dans les trois romans que je viens de citer, ne reproduit-elle pas, dans l'ensemble et en mille variations nouvelles, celle de Saint-Preux dans la seconde partie l'*Héloïse*?" *Ibid.*, p. 65. Consult also, Edmond Vermeil "La Nouvelle Héloïse et son influence sur l'oeuvre de Goethe," *Colloque international sur Goethe et l'esprit français* (Strasbourg, 1957), *Actes*, (Paris, 1958), pp. 57–68.

15. Jacques Voisine, *J.-J. Rousseau en Angleterre à l'époque romantique* (Paris, 1956), p. 221. "Il n'est donc pas question de voir en Wordsworth un disciple de la philosophie rousseauiste. Mais s'il s'écarte de Rousseau penseur, il est par certains côtés singulièrement proche de Rousseau poète, du Rousseau des *Confessions* et des *Rêveries*. D'une part, il semble avoir saisi le lien qui fait des *Confessions*, en un sens, le prolongement de *l'Emile*: l'idée de la continuité du développement psychologique, qui fait de l'éducation le travail de toute une vie: l'idée protestante de l'énergie intérieure et de l'éducation de l'homme par lui-même; idée féconde que doivent au premier chef à Rousseau

les auteurs d'*Erziehungs-* ou *Bildungsromane* dans l'Allemagne du début du XIX siècle." And in an earlier study "L'influence de la *Nouvelle Héloïse* sur la génération de *Werther*" in *Etudes Germaniques,* Nos. 2–3, Avril-Septembre, 1950, p. 130, he concludes his important essay as follows: "Le roman de Rousseau, dont l'influence se combinera avec celle de son traité d'éducation, sera à la source d'un puissant courant à la fois moral et poétique; c'est en grande partie grâce à Rousseau que se développera dans le romantisme allemand l'idée féconde de l'éducation de l'homme par lui-même et par la vie. La conception rousseauiste du développement d'une âme, avec ses élans et ses chutes, et de sa victoire sur elle-même, se retrouvera, élargie, débarassée des éléments extérieurs, dans le *Titan* de Jean-Paul, le *Wilhelm Meister* de Goethe, le *Heinrich von Ofterdingen* de Novalis, et d'autres grandes oeuvres encore illustrant plus particulièrement le thème de la formation du poète."

16. Schopenhauer, *Werke, Die Welt als Wille und Vorstellung,* (Brockhaus, München, 1960), I, p. 220.

17. By way of example, one should quote Rousseau, who relates in his *Confessions* the reactions of Thérèse's mother to the first readings of *La Nouvelle Héloïse:* "Tous les soirs aux coin de mon feu je lisois et relisois ces deux Parties aux Gouverneuses. La Fille sans rien dire sanglotoit avec moi d'attendrissement; la mere, qui ne trouvant point là de compliment, n'y comprenoit rien, restoit tranquille, et se contentoit dans les momens de silence de me répéter toujours: *Monsieur, cela est bien beau.*" (I, 436).

18. Schopenhauer, *Werke, Parerga und Paralipomena,* (Stuttgart, 1965), V, p. 520. Hamann, an early admirer of Rousseau, writes concerning the latter's conception of the novel: "Vielleicht hat Rousseau die wahre Natur des Romanhaften tiefer eingesehen und glücklicher nachgeahmt, dass seine Geschicklichkeit hierin ein unvergebliches Verbrechen in den Augen solcher Virtuosen seyn mag, denen ihr Gewissen über ihre Muster dunkele Vorwürfe macht." "Abälardus Viribus an den Verfasser der fünf Briefe die neue Heloise betreffend" *Kreuzzüge eines Philologen, SW,* II (Vienna, 1950), pp. 161, 2. Curiously enough, Friedrich Schlegel considers *La Nouvelle Héloïse a roman à idée:* "Voltaire, Rousseau und Diderot bedienten sich also oft des Romans ganz willkürlich, bloss als einer Form, um gewisse eigentümliche Ideen, die sich in keine andere Form so gut fügen wollten, wider zu legen." Friedrich Schlegel, *Kritische Ausgabe* (München, 1961), VI, 1st part, p. 331.

19. Victor Lange, preface to *Wilhelm Meister's Apprenticeship,* transl. by Carlyle, (New York, 1968), p. 10.

20. Cf. Homer, *The Odyssey,* transl. by Richmond Lattimore, New York, 1965), Bk I, 11.296,7: Pallas Athena speaking to Telemachus: ". . . You should not go on clinging to your childhood. You are no longer of an age to do that."

21. Karl Schlechta, *Goethes Wilhelm Meister* (Frankfurt, 1953), p. 57.

22. Cf. Robert Osmont, "Remarques sur la genèse et la composition de la *Nouvelle Héloïse,* in *ASJJR,* XXXIII (1953–55), p. 148: "C'est en écrivant la *Nouvelle Héloïse* que Rousseau a découvert le mystère du temps et de la destinée."

23. Ernst Cassirer, *Rousseau, Kant, Goethe* (Princeton, 1947), p. 14.

24. Kurt May " 'Wilhelm Meisters Lehrjahre,' ein Bildungsroman?" *Dvjs,* XXXI, 1957, p. 36.

25. *Ibid.,* p. 37.

26. It is worthwhile to make a textual comparison between Goethe's description and Rousseau's evocation of Clarens: ". . . ce n'est plus une maison faite pour être vue, mais pour être habitée . . . Tout y est agréable et riant; tout y respire l'abondance et la propreté, rien n'y sent la richesse et le luxe. Il n'y a pas une chambre où l'on ne se reconnoisse à la campagne, et où l'on ne

retrouve toutes les comodités de la ville. Les mêmes changemens se font re-
marquer au dehors . . . Aux tristes Ifs qui couvroient les murs ont été
substitués de bons espaliers. Au lieu de l'inutile maronier d'Inde, de jeunes
meuriers noirs commencent à ombrager la cour, et l'on a planté deux rangs de
noyers jusqu'au chemin à la place des vieux tilleuls qui bordoient l'avenue.
Par tout on a substitué l'utile à l'agréable, et l'agréable y a presque toujours
gagné." (II, 441, 2). Here is the countryseat of the Oberamtmann: "Der Oberamtmann . . . hatte nach eignem Blick und Einsicht, nach Liebhaberei seiner Frau, ja
zuletzt nach Wünschen und Grillen seiner Kinder erst grössere und kleinere
abgesonderte Anlagen besorgt und begünstigt, welche, mit Gefühl allmählich
durch Pflanzungen und Wege verbunden, eine allerliebste, verschiedentlich
abweichende, charakteristische Szenenfolge dem Durchwandelnden darstellten
. . . Die nächste so wie die fernere Gegend war zu bescheidenen Anlagen und
eigentlich ländlichen Einzelheiten höchst geeignet . . . und wenn Grund und
Boden vorzüglich dem Nutzen gewidmet erschien, so war doch das Anmutige,
das Reizende nicht ausgeschlossen. An die Haupt-und Wirtschaftsgebäude
fügten sich Lust-, Obst- und Grasgärtchen, aus denen man sich unversehens in
ein Hölzchen verlor, das ein breiter, fahrbarer Weg auf und ab, hin und wider
durchschlängelte" (VIII, 93, 4). Which *rousseauiste* does not recognize *le petit
bosquet?* Even more striking than the concordances between *La Nouvelle
Héloïse* and *Wilhelm Meisters Wanderjahre* are the affinities between M. de
Wolmar and Saint-Preux on the one hand and, on the other, Heinrich
Drendorf and his Gastfreund *(Der Nachsommer)*: "La patience et le temps, dit
M. de Wolmar, ont fait ce miracle. Ce sont des expédiens dont les gens riches
ne s'avisent gueres dans leurs plaisirs . . . ils ont des oiseaux dans des cages . . .
On ne les fait pas venir quand il n'y en a point, mais il est aisé quand il y
en a d'en attirer davantage en prévenant tous leurs besoins, en ne les effrayant
jamais, en leur laissant faire leur couvée en sûreté et ne dénichant point les
petits . . ." (II, 476). Still, serene, soundless like Jean-Jacques' meditations,
Stifter's disquisitions under the sign *des sanften Gesetzes* render in the German
mood the universal intuition of life in its pure state, uncontaminated by will
and desire. " 'Wie kann man den einen Vogel schützen?' fragte ich. 'Ihn kann
man nicht schützen,' sagte mein Gastfreund, er schützt sich selber; aber die
Gelegenheit zum Schutze kann man ihm geben . . . Will man Vögel in eine
Gegend ziehen, so muss man solche Zufluchtsorte schaffen, und zwar so gut
als möglich. Wir können, wie Ihr seht, nicht Felsen und Baumstämme
aushöhlen, aber aus Holz gemachte Höhlungen können wir überall auf die
Bäume aufhängen. Und dies tun wir auch . . . 'Ich habe sie gesehen,' erwiderte
ich, 'habe dunkel vermutet, wozu sie dienen könnten . . .' " *Der Nachsommer*
(München, 1961), p. 109.

27. The first one to relate the hero of the *Bildungsroman* to Leibnitz'
philosophy is Max Wundt, *op. cit.*, p. 7.

28. To what degree *Wilhelm Meisters Lehrjahre* embodies a direct influence
of *La Nouvelle Héloïse* in particular, and Rousseau's immense affective and
ideological influence in general, is a very complex question not within the
compass of this essay which, by confining itself to suggesting structural and
thematic analogies between the two novels, has attempted to clarify their relationship to one another in the light of the concept of the *Bildungsroman*. For
general background material, consult "Rousseau et le mouvement philosophique
en Allemagne" by I. Benrubi in *ASJJR*, VIII, 1912, pp. 99–130. For a general
bibliography and treatment of the question, see also Guthke, "Zur Frühgeschichte des Rousseauismus in Deutschland" in *Zeitschrift für deutsche
Philologie*, vol. 77, 1958, pp. 284–397. See also: M. Temmer, *Time in Rousseau
and Kant*, (Geneva, 1958). Consult also bibliographical reference vol. edited by
ASJJR. Goethe's own testimony regarding *La Nouvelle Héloïse* is as scarce as

it is suggestive; seventeen years before the publication of *Wilhelm Meisters Lehrjahre*, he writes to Frau von Stein on October 23, 1779: "Wir fuhren nach Veway, ich konnte mich der Tränen nicht enthalten, wenn ich nach Melleraye [La Meillerie] hinüber sahe und den *dent de Chamant* und die ganzen Plätze vor mir hatte, die der ewig einsame Rousseau mit empfindenden Wesen bevölckerte" (*Werke*, Weimar, 1889, IV Abt., vol. IV, p. 93). In the past, most studies that dealt with the problem of the influence of France on Goethe, either reduced the problem "Goethe-Rousseau" to a few platitudes, or followed the course indicated by Erich Schmidt. Surprisingly, Fritz Strich's *Goethe and World Literature* belongs to the first group; his index refers to Rousseau five times only, and his lengthiest statement informs the reader ". . . that there is no doubt . . . that Swiss literature, Rousseau and Haller and Gessner, played a very important part in awakening Goethe to consciousness of himself and his own nature" (*Goethe and World Literature* London, 1949, p. 87). The second group of scholars, led by Hippolyte Loiseau, elaborates the suggestions by Erich Schmidt. Thus, Loiseau's *Goethe et la France* resounds with the name of Rousseau, but concludes that ". . . le rapprochement [entre *La Nouvelle Héloïse* et *Werther*] n'est plus qu'affaire de curiosité d'histoire littéraire et d'ingéniosité critique (Paris, 1931, p. 328). Fritz Neubert, discussing French antecedents of *Wilhelm Meister*, limits himself to emphasizing "die kräftige Anregung, die er [Goethe] für die ersten fünf Bücher seines *Wilhelm Meister* durch den derblustigen *Roman comique* Scarrons erfuhr" (*Studien zur vergleichenden Literaturgeschichte, Festgabe* [Berlin, 1951] p. 67). Far more instructive than any preceding work on the problem of the relationships between Goethe and French literature and Goethe and *La Nouvelle Héloïse* are studies by Albert Fuchs and Edmond Vermeil which appeared in *Goethe et l'esprit français* (Paris, 1958). Indeed, Vermeil's article, which must be considered *grundlegend* for any future evaluations of relationships between Goethe's novels and *La Nouvelle Héloïse*, restates, in the main, his views already analyzed above (cf. his article in *Les Annales de la Société J.-J. Rousseau* 1946–49). Fuchs' article, sophisticated and synthetic, is a brilliant *mise au point* of Goethe's attitudes towards France and its artists, writers, and thinkers. Mention should also be made of Kurt Wais' article "Goethe und Frankreich" in *Dvjs*, XXIII, 1949, p. 472–500. In it, he states concerning Goethe's *Frankreicherlebnis*: "Vor allem lässt sich an Rousseau denken. Was Goethe mit Lotte und ihrem Verlobten erlebte, berührt sich äusserlich damit, wie in Rousseaus berühmten Briefroman der entsagende Liebhaber Saint-Preux seiner Julie und ihrem edlen Gatten gegenübertritt. Indessen gibt es in 'Werther' nichts, worin eine Nachahmung der 'Neuen Heloise' wirklich greifbar würde" *Ibid.*, 474.

29. Jung and Kerényi, *Essays on a Science of Mythology* (Princeton, 1949), p. 25.

30. Wilamowitz-Moellendorff, *Die Heimkehr des Odysseus* (Berlin, 1927), p. 106.

31. Werner Jaeger, *Paideia—The Ideals of Greek Culture*, transl. from the second German ed. by Gilbert Highet (New York, 1945), p. 29.

32. Howard Clarke, *American Journal of Philology*, LXXXIV, 2, p. 133.

33. Erich Auerbach, *Mimesis* (Princeton, 1953), p. 25.

34. *Ibid.*, p. 33.

35. *Ibid.*, p. 35.

36. Claudio Guillén, his preface to *Lazarillo de Tormes* (New York, 1966), p. 12.

37. Odette de Mourgues, *Racine or the Triumph of Relevance* (Cambridge, 1966), p. 83.

38. Seneca *Tragédies, Medea*, (Paris, 1961, Budé), 11.171, 2 and 1.910.

39. It is worthwhile to note that Sartre's *Les Mains sales* which exhibits

structural dramatic analogies with *Cinna* (Hoederer-Auguste, Hugo-Cinna, Jessica-Emilie) rejects the necessity of maturation, *ergo Bildung*: Cf. Hoederer "La jeunesse, je ne sais pas ce que c'est: je suis passé directement de l'enfance à l'âge d'homme." Hugo: "Oui. C'est une maladie bourgeoise. Il y en a beaucoup qui en meurent" (Quatrième Tableau, Sc. III).

40. Concerning Rousseau's role in European letters, it is well to remember Joseph Texte's *Jean-Jacques Rousseau et les origines du cosmopolitisme littéraire* (Paris, 1895) which concludes with the following remark pertinent to this discussion (p. 459): "J'ai essayé de montrer qu'entre l'Europe du Nord et la France, un homme surtout a servi de lien; que, préparé par ses origines étrangères au rôle de médiateur et d'initiateur, et admirablement servi d'ailleurs par son éducation en pays de langue française, il a été puissamment aidé par les circonstances dans l'accomplissement de cette tâche; que son esprit— le plus complexe et le plus riche de son siècle—a vraiment provoqué la naissance d'une sorte de littérature européenne, dont l'avenir est désormais assuré; que s'il n'a pas, enfin, réussi à déplacer l'hégémonie littéraire de l'Europe aux dépens de la France latine et au profit des nations du Nord, il a du moins fait comprendre à l'une le génie original des autres et qu'il a, par là, mérité la reconnaissance de toutes.

41. Bernard Schilling (*The Hero as Failure,* Chicago, 1968) considers *Illusions perdues* as a *Bildungsroman* without, however, taking into account the element of the self-generating ethos or, for that matter, the literature on the subject-matter.

42. Flaubert, *Corresp.,* (Conard, 1910), IV, p. 400, lettre du 6 oct., 1864, à Mlle Leroyer de Chantepie.

43. Regarding the fortunes of *La Nouvelle Héloïse* in England during the Romantic Age, consult Jacques Voisine, *op. cit.* For the relationship between *Wilhelm Meister* and some 19th century English authors, see Susanne Howe, *Wilhelm Meister and his English Kinsmen* (New York, 1906). Consult also: Hans Wagner, *Der englische Bildungsroman bis in die Zeit des ersten Weltkrieges* (Bern, 1951).

44. Joseph Conrad, *Lord Jim,* ed. by T. Moser (New York, 1968), p. 8.

45. *Ibid.,* p. 32.

46. Analyzing the influence of *La Nouvelle Héloïse* in terms of its treatment of *le temps vécu,* Professor Voisine writes: "On pourrait peut-être sans trop d'arbitraire retracer la filiation de l'auteur de la *Nouvelle Héloïse* à George Eliot, en passant par Wordsworth et Hazlitt, et celle de George Eliot, par Marcel Proust, à des romanciers contemporains comme Virginia Woolf, Aldous Huxley ou Charles Morgan . . ." *Op. cit.,* p. 438. Somerset Maugham's *Of Human Bondage* might also be interpreted as a *Bildungsroman.*

Footnotes to Chapter IV

1. Unless indicated otherwise, all references to Gottfried Keller's works relate to the Fränkel and Helbing edition of his *Sämtliche Werke* (Bern, 1926–42). Roman numerals refer to volumes. All references in Arabic numerals to Rousseau's *Confessions* relate to the pagination of *Les œuvres complètes*, vol. I, edited by Bernard Gagnebin and Marcel Raymond (Pléiade, 1959). Whenever possible references to Rousseau and Keller have been integrated into the text.

2. *Gottfried Kellers Briefe und Tagebücher,* ed. Emil Ermatinger (Stuttgart and Berlin 1916), 2nd ed., vol. II, p. 323.

3. *Ibid.,* vol. III, p. 222. Another allusion to Rousseau not mentioned in this

essay may be found in the 1865 edition of *Die missbrauchten Liebesbriefe* in which there is a reference to Julie von Bondeli's defense of *La Nouvelle Héloïse* in 1761 (cf. vol. VIII, Notes, pp. 465–70). Another such reference is located in *Das Sinngedicht*, chap. xii, "Die Berlocken" (XI, 328). Keller's "Verfassungsrevision in Zürich," in 1864 (XXI, 172), contains a short reference to Rousseau's *Considérations sur le gouvernement de Pologne* and his *Projet de constitution pour la Corse*.

4. Therese Seiler, *Gottfried Keller und die französische Literatur* (Zürich, 1955), p. 32. Miss Seiler does not even mention Georg Lukács' book on *Gottfried Keller* (Berlin, 1946) in which he discusses Rousseau and Keller. The only other major confrontation of Keller and a French author is by Norbert Fürst, "The Structure of 'l'Education Sentimentale' and 'Der grüne Heinrich,'" in *PMLA*, 1956, pp. 249–60. The one scholar who could and should have related *Der grüne Heinrich* to the *Confessions* was Fernand Baldensperger, who limits himself to this unfortunate comparison: "Quoi qu'il en soit, et indépendamment de son intérêt déguisé—une autobiographie de sincérité et qui n'a point l'outrance dans l'aveu par où s'épanche le cœur présomptueux et ulcéré de Rousseau, ni cette façon d'enluminer ses actions par où Goethe tend à laisser de soi une image retouchée,—c'est à ce titre de roman éducatif qu'*Henri le Vert* est surtout caractéristique et qu'il a sa place toute marquée dans les traditions de la prose allemande. Car c'est une forme excellemment allemande que celle de l'Ichroman . . ." *Gottfried Keller. Sa vie et ses oeuvres* (Paris, 1899), p. 154.

5. Quoted by E. Ermatinger, *Gottfried Kellers Leben* (Zürich, 1950), p. 212.

6. M. Cornicelius, "Romanische Einflüsse in Gottfried Kellers Dichtung" in *Festschrift für Adolf Tobler* (Braunschweig, 1905), pp. 117–136.

7. William Harrison Faulkner, "Keller's *Der grüne Heinrich*: Anna and Judith and their predecessors in Rousseau's *Confessions*," *University of Virginia Publications Bulletin of the Philosophical Society—Humanistic Section*, vol. I, No. 2, Feb. 1912, pp. 51–57.

8. "Es wäre eine flache Erklärung dieses Gegensatzes, wollte man in Keller nur den Künstler sehen, und bei Rousseau den politischen Theoretiker und Publizisten einseitig in den Vordergrund stellen. Denn einmal bildet das theoretische und künstlerische Lebenswerk Rousseaus eine unzertrennbare Einheit, die als solche Einheit zur welthistorischen Wirksamkeit gelangt ist. Man kann seine Romane, seine Selbstbiographie usw. nicht von dem 'Gesellschaftsvertrag' absondern. Und wenn die Einheit dieses Lebenswerkes eine widerspruchvolle gewesen ist, so hat es gerade durch diesen inneren Widerspruch einheitlich und als Ganzes gewirkt. Denn dieser Widerspruch war der des Lebens . . . Zum andern könnte Keller nur sehr bedingt als blosser Künstler gelten. Seine fünfzehnjährige Tätigkeit auf dem hohen und verantwortlichen Posten als Staatsschreiber der Zürcher Demokratie (1851/1876) ist keineswegs eine bloss biographische Episode. Der grosse autobiographische Jugendroman Kellers, 'Der grüne Heinrich,' hat die Erziehung eines vielseitigen und problematischen Menschen zur öffentlichen, zur politischen Tätigkeit als Grundthema . . . Erziehung zur öffentlichen Wirksamkeit: das ist der leitende Grundgedanke der ganzen schriftstellerischen Tätigkeit Kellers." Lukács, *op. cit.*, pp. 27, 28.

9. See Melitta Gerhard, *Der deutsche Entwicklungsroman bis zu Goethes Wilhelm Meister* (Halle, 1926). For a more recent and less rigid view, see Kurt May, "*Wilhelm Meisters Lehrjahre*, ein Bildungsroman?" *Deutsche Vierteljahrsschrift für Literatur und Geisteswissenschaft*, vol. 31, 1957, pp. 1–37.

10. Ermatinger, "Keller und Goethe," *PMLA*, LXIV, 1949, p. 87. For the relationship between Rousseau's *La Nouvelle Héloïse* and Goethe's *Wilhelm Meisters Lehrjahre*, see chapter 3 in this volume.

11. *Ibid.,* p. 89.

12. Agnes Waldhausen, "Gottfried Kellers Grüner Heinrich in seinen Beziehungen zu Goethes Dichtung und Wahrheit," *Euphorion,* 1909, XVI, pp. 471–97.

13. Quoted by Martin Sommerfeld, *Goethe in Umwelt und Folgezeit,* Jean-Jacques Rousseaus "Bekenntnisse" und Goethes "Dichtung und Wahrheit" (Leiden, 1935), p. 12.

14. Quoted by Ermatinger, p. 302.

15. Hugo von Hofmannsthal, *Gesammelte Werke,* Prosa II, Frankfurt, 1959, p. 166.

16. Frieda Jaeggi, *Gottfried Keller und Jean Paul* (Bern, 1913).

17. Walter Muschg, "Gottfried Keller und Jeremias Gotthelf," in *Jahrbuch des freien deutschen Hochstifts,* 1936–40, pp. 159–98.

18. Rudolf Majut, "Der deutsche Roman von Biedermeier bis zur Gegenwart," in Wolfgang Stammler, *Deutsche Philologie im Aufriss* (Berlin, 1958), II, p. 1509.

19. Barker Fairley, *Der grüne Heinrich* (Oxford, 1943), Introd., p. 47.

20. *Ibid.,* p. 52.

21. *Ibid.*

22. *Ibid.*

23. Sommerfeld, *op. cit.,* pp. 14, 15. On autobiography, consult standard works by George Misch, *Geschichte der Autobiographie* (Bern, 1948–67); Roy Pascal, *Design and Truth in Autobiography* (Cambridge, 1960); also excellent articles respectively by Georg Gusdorf, "Conditions et limites de l'autobiographie" in *Formen der Selbstdarstellung, Festgabe für Fritz Neubert,* ed. Reichenkron and Haas (Berlin, 1956), pp. 105–23, and by Jacques Voisine, "Naissance et évolution du terme littéraire 'autobiographie'" in *La Littérature comparée en Europe orientale, Conférence de Budapest* (Budapest, 1963), pp. 278–86. See also Jacques Voisine's introduction to his edition of *Les Confessions* (Paris, Garnier), 1964.

24. Saint Augustine, *Confessiones,* edited and transl. by Pierre de Labriolle, éd. Guillaume Budé (Paris, 1961), Liber Decimus, VIII, vol. 2, p. 248.

25. Goethe, *Werke, Maximen und Reflexionen* (Hamburg, 1966), vol. XII, p. 413.

26. *Op. cit.,* 134.

27. For Keller, crystalline transparency is the highest quality of any representation of man and his world, and he attributes it to Shakespeare; see *Pankraz der Schmoller,* VII, 50. Consult also, Starobinski, *J. J. Rousseau, La transparence et l'obstacle* (Paris, 1957). Keller's comment originates probably in Goethe's remarks on Shakespeare in *Wilhelm Meister Lehrjahre,* Werke, vol. VII, p. 192.

28. Goethe, *Werke,* vol. V, *Tasso,* Act. II, Sc. 3, line 1239, Antonio speaking.

29. Letter to Wilhelm Petersen, April 21, 1881, *Gottfried Kellers Briefe und Tagebücher,* vol. III, p. 347.

30. Needless to emphasize that there are numerous interpretations of this *Grundtrauer.* Among the livelier ones, one has to mention Majut's view: "Wenn irgendwo, so ist im Falle des 'Grünen Heinrich' das tiefenpsychologische Schlagwort 'Komplex' am Platze, wie sich denn auch die psychoanalytischen Wühlmäuse mit weitaus grösserem Recht an Keller herangemacht haben als (besonders in Amerika) an Goethe. (E. Hitschmann, *Gottfried Keller, Psychoanalyse des Dichters, seiner Gestalten und Motive,* 1919). Heinrich ist einer des gebrochensten Charaktere in der Gesamtgeschichte des deutschen Romans, ein schweizer Naturbursche voll natürlicher Lebensfreude, der zu jedem normalen Glück unfähig ist, ein in seinem starken Willen Unbeugsamer, der sich bis zur Haltlosigkeit treiben lässt . . . Sein Leben ist keine Komödie der

Irrungen, sondern der Hemmungen, was sich besonders an seinem Verhältnis zu den Frauen versinnbildlicht." *Op. cit.*, p. 1509. Rudolf Wildholf turns this *Grundtrauer* into *Daseinsnot*: "Wer aus vielfältig erlittener Daseinsnot nach der Möglichkeit der Bewältigung fragt und zeit seines Lebens nicht aufhört, aus diesem nie verdeckten Ursprung heraus zu fragen, für den ist das Dasein seinem Wesen nach nicht völlig in sich rund und gewiss. Keller ist nicht der Dichter des heilen Daseins, so wenig als des verlorenen. Seine Stellung liegt in der Mitte." *Gottfried Kellers Menschenbild* (Bern, 1965), p. 15. Leopold Ziegler writes: "Es [das Wort] fällt in einen Brunnenschacht von nicht zu ermessender Tiefe—unfern vielleicht dem Urquell also doch, der 'rechte' Freude mit der 'Grundtrauer' gemeinsam speist und spendet . . ." *Dreiflügelbild—Keller, Pestalozzi, Stifter* (München, 1961). p. 39.

31. Marcel Raymond, his introd. to *Les Confessions*, p. xv.

32. A passage from a letter to Salomon Hegi, dated Zürich, April 1, 1843, suggests that the *Confessions* and *La Nouvelle Héloïse* must have been among Keller's *livres de chevet*: "Zugleich schicke mir eine genaue Rechnung, da es wahrscheinlich ziemlich mehr als 80 Gulden ausmachen wird; wozu noch der versetzte Meerschaum, Benvenuto Cellini und Rousseaus 'Héloïse' und 'Confessions' zu rechnen sind, die ich, während Du im Tirol warst, an einem mageren Tage verkaufte und vor meiner Abreise bei keinem Antiquar mehr fand." *Gottfried Kellers Briefe und Tagebücher*, II, p. 96. It is regrettable that these or other copies of Rousseau's works at one time in Keller's possession have been lost; the ones at the *Zentralbibliothek* in Zürich show no markings or signs of having been read. In his letter to Hettner, June 26, 1854, Keller discusses his reading of St. Augustine's *Confessions*: "Ich lese jetzt die Bekenntnisse des heiligen Augustinus, welche auch nichts anderes sind als eine geistige Robinsonade, nämlich insofern man zuschaut, wie sich ein Individuum alles neu erwerben, aneignen und sich einrichten muss." After expostulating on thematic resemblances between Tieck's "Die Reisenden" and the second book of Pantagruel, chap. 11, Keller attacks "die Herren Romantiker" for pretending originality: "Man sollte allen Leuten, welche anfangen wollen, sich mit der *Produktion* zu befassen, dringend raten, durchaus allen vorhandenen Stoff systematisch durchzulesen und so mit allen eitlen Einbildungen, als würden sie neu sein, *Tabula rasa* zu machen. Es bringt nun zwar mancher ein Motiv oder eine Manier aufs Tapet, welches er wirklich nirgends gelesen hat, und das doch schon alt ist. In solchen Fällen glaubt man sich gerade schmeicheln zu dürfen, auf das verfallen zu sein, worauf früher schon bessere Leute, ohne doch etwas davon zu wissen." The passage ends with a doubt concerning Cervantes' originality in his execution (*Ausführung*) of *Don Quijote*. Why then Keller's surprising reticence concerning Rousseau's *Confessions*? The answer may be implicit in his angry denunciation of Tieck. Anger is the effective characteristic of this letter, in which he goes on to accuse Paul Heyse of *Goethetuerei*, absolving him, however, by virture of his youth: ". . . möchten doch alle, welche ihm die Zukunft absprechen, sich erinnern, was *sie* eigentlich in jenem Alter gemacht *nachgeahmt* haben . . ." (Keller's italics). Similarly, Mosenthal is called to task for having availed himself in his *Sonnenwendhof* of Gotthelfian motives: "Es ist, wie im 'Struensee', eine mit echt jüdischer Gemeinheit und Frechheit zusammengestoppelte Sammlung kleiner Effektchen, die auf alle Schwächen des Publikums *spekulieren*." *Ibid.*, vol. II, pp. 347–49.

33. M. Temmer, *Time in Rousseau and Kant* (Geneva, 1958). Also consult chapter I of this volume which treats Rousseau's technique in suggesting the passage of time.

34. Emil Staiger, *Die Zeit als Einbildungskraft des Dichters* (Zürich, 1963), p. 171 ff.

35. *Ibid.*, p. 179 ff.

36. Gaston Bachelard, *La terre et les rêveries du repos* (Paris, 1948), p. 119.

37. St. Augustine, *Confessiones*, II, XI, p. 26.

38. Admittedly, the word "to paint" has to be used with considerable caution. Cf. Wolfgang Preisendanz' remarks: "Dabei gibt es von den Malversuchen kaum einen Zugang zu den im Medium der Sprache gegebenen Bildvorstellungen; das bequeme Schlagwort vom Malerauge versperrte lange genug die Erkenntnis der viel eher aus der frühen Lyrik kommenden Ursprünge und der Besonderheit einer ganz auf die Eigengesetzlichkeit der Sprache angewiesenen Bildgestaltung im Werke des Erzählers." "Die Keller-Forschung der Jahre 1939–1957" in *GRM*, 39/2, p. 150.

39. Jean Paul Richter, *Werke* (München, 1963), vol. VI, p. 1048.

40. Cornicelius, p. 122.

41. *Ibid.*, p. 124.

42. W. Guggenheim holds a similar view in that he considers Keller's celibacy not so much the result of his failures in love as an expression of his desire for artistic freedom: "Das Versagen-Müssen wird sinnfällig, sinnvoll. Um des Werkes willen." *Das Ende von Seldwyla* (Zürich, 1965), p. 39.

43. Rousseau, *Correspondance générale*, éd. T. Dufour (Paris, 1927), vol. VII, p. 72. *Lettres à M. de Malesherbes*, le 26 janvier 1762.

44. A propos, Ricarda Huch writes: "In vielen Fällen verleiht Keller den Frauen eine gewisse Überlegenheit den Männern gegenüber, die als gute, leidenschaftliche Wesen, nach altgermanischer Auffassung, ihrer Harmonie und Besonnenheit bedürfen." *Gottfried Keller* (Berlin-Leipzig, 1905), p. 59.

45. Faulkner, p. 57.

46. Ermatinger, p. 57. Concerning the theme of the *Doppelliebe*, consult articles by Edmond Vermeil, "Goethe et Rousseau" in *ASJJR*, XXXI, 1946–49, pp. 57–77, and "*La Nouvelle Héloïse* et son influence sur l'œuvre de Goethe" in *Colloque International sur Goethe et l'Esprit Français* (Paris, 1958), pp. 57–68.

47. *Les rêveries du promeneur solitaire—Xe Promenade* in *Les Confessions—Autres textes autobiographiques* (Paris, 1959), p. 1098.

48. Letter to Theodor Storm, June 25, 1878. *Briefe und Tagebücher*, vol. III, p. 247.

49. Despite Majut's sharp attack against Hitschmann and psychoanalysis in general, I refer the indulgent reader to the latter's book, which states "obvious truths" long before anyone else thought of them: "Dem Laien weniger plausibel, dem Psychoanalytiker aber aus Erfahrung voll beweiskräftig ist ein häufiger symbolischer Gebrauch des Apfels bei Keller: Der Apfel ist in Mythus und Märchen ein Symbol der Frauenbrust, schon in der Verführungsszene zwischen Adam und Eva. Judith im *Grünen Heinrich*— wie wir noch ausführen werden: eine Ersatzgestalt der Mutter—tritt auf mit einer 'Last frisch gepflückter Ernteäpfel', holt dann Milch herbei und hält Heinrich das Gefäss an den Mund. Er schlürft mit 'unbeschreiblichem Behagen' den 'marmorweissen Trunk'." *Op. cit.*, p. 23, 4 ff. Rousseau's concern with bosoms is too well known (cf. his remarks about Mme d'Epinay, *Conf.*, Pt. I, Bk. IX) to deserve mention. Less known, however, is his vision of country festivals whose ingredients will be the same in Keller's chapters on Glattfelden: "Dans les maisons j'imaginois des festins rustiques, dans les près de folâtres jeux, le long des eaux, les bains, des promenades, la pêche, sur les arbres des fruits délicieux, sous leurs ombres de voluptueux tête-à-têtes, sur les montagnes des cuves de lait et de crème . . ." (p. 58). On Rousseau's interest in milk, consult Gagnebin's commentary in "Notes et Variantes," *op. cit.*, p. 1261.

50. On Keller and Gessner, consult Rita Buser, *Gottfried Keller und Salomon Gessner* (Liestal, Basel, 1963).

51. "Es waren verschiedene Briefe von Paris gekommen. Rousseau schrieb

Herrn Huber, einem Übersetzer Gessners, die schmeichelhaftesten Dinge über letzteren, und wie er dessen Werke nicht mehr aus der Hand lege. Diderot wünschte sogar, einige seiner Erzählungen mit den neuesten Idyllen Gessners in einem Bande gemeinschaftlich erscheinen zu lassen. Dass Rousseau für den idealen Naturzustand jener idyllischen Welt schwärmte, war am Ende nichts Wunderbares, dass aber der grosse Realist und Enzyklopädist nach dem Vergnügen strebte, mit dem harmlosen Idyllendichter Arm in Arm aufzutreten, erschien als die erdenklich wichtigste Ergänzung des Lobes und gab zum Verdrusse Gessners Anlass zu den breitesten Erörterungen" (IX, 200, 201). Keller's source for this passage is J. J. Hottinger, *Salomon Gessner* (Zürich, 1798).

52. Schiller, *Werke, Über naive und sentimentalische Dichtung* (Frankfurt, 1966), vol. IV, p. 339.

53. Jean Paul Richter, *Werke—Vorschule der Aesthetik*, vol. V, p. 258. Concerning Jean Paul and Rousseau, consult Edward Berend, *Jean Paul und die Schweiz* (Frauenfeld and Leipzig, 1943).

54. Friedrich Theodor Vischer, *Kritische Gänge* (München, 1922), vol. VI, p. 265.

55. The question of Rousseau's influence on Keller in the area of the history of ideas remains to be studied, including the transmission to Keller of Rousseau's ontological and existential concepts through Fichte, Hegel, and Feuerbach. Consult also the precise article by Karl S. Guthke, "Zur Frühgeschichte des Rousseauismus in Deutschland" in *Zeitschrift für deutsche Philologie*, vol. 77, 1958, pp. 384–96, which contains a useful bibliography. For the relationship between Rousseau and the German Idealists, see standard works by Cassirer, Gurvitch, as well as Jean Hyppolite's translation of, and commentary on, Hegel's *Phenomenology of Mind*. For a partial bibliography, see M. Temmer, *Time in Rousseau and Kant*, chap. v. There are still other points of contact between Rousseau and Keller: their passion for *la fête populaire*, their views on money and its uses, their love of wandering (cf. K. S. Guthke, "Das Motiv des Wanderers bei Gottfried Keller in der Romantik" in *Wege Zur Literatur*, Bern, 1967, pp. 187–97). A further subject of investigation is their participation in Swiss cultural values and ideals, as for example the question of ethical realism in *La Nouvelle Héloïse* and *Der grüne Heinrich* (cf. Karl Fehr, *Der Realismus in der schweizerischen Literatur*, Bern, 1956, and François Jost, *Jean-Jacques Rousseau—Suisse* (Fribourg, 1961), 2 vol. and *Essais de littérature comparée* (Fribourg, 1964).

56. Adolf Frey, *Erinnerungen an Gottfried Keller* (Leipzig, 1919), pp. 32, 33: Frey's remarks concerning Keller's supposed gratitude towards other authors strike a curious note: "Gegen lebende und tote Dichter, deren fördernden Einfluss er je empfunden, beseelte ihn eine unwandelbare Dankbarkeit."

57. This is true to the point that the old Keller could write to Theodor Storm concerning Judith: "Ihm [Heinrich] ist sie das Beste, was er erlebt hat . . ." Letter of June 25, 1878, *Briefe und Tagebücher*, vol. III, p. 247. Rousseau could never have subscribed to such a subordination of life to literature—so characteristic of the nineteenth century (cf. Mallarmé ". . . le monde n'est qu'un prétexte pour un beau livre.")—especially in the realm of autobiography: "Pourquoi m'ôter le charme actuel de la jouissance pour dire à d'autres que j'avois joui? Que m'importoient des lecteurs un public et toute la terre, tandis que je plânois dans le Ciel?" (p. 162). Furthermore, one should note that Keller was deeply concerned with the relationship between his experiences, *his* book, i.e., *Der grüne Heinrich* and his readers as well as with the ensuing problem of integrating harmoniously the factors of writing, living, and earning a livelihood; and it is no accident that he turned to Spinoza and Rousseau to illustrate his, that is to say, Heinrich's dilemma. In the first ver-

sion of *Der grüne Heinrich*, he opposes Spinoza and Rousseau as symbols of the split and inorganic life to Schiller, representative of the unified organic life: "Gegenüber diesem einheitlichen organischen Leben gibt es nun auch ein gespaltenes, getrenntes, gewissermassen unorganisches Leben, wie wenn Spinoza und Rousseau grosse Denker sind in ihrem innern Berufe nach und, um sich zu ernähren, zugleich Brillengläser schleifen und Noten schreiben. Diese Art beruht auf einer Entsagung, welche in Ausnahmsfällen dem selbstbewussten Menschen wohl ansteht, als Zeugnis seiner Gewalt" (XIX, 82). In the second version, Rousseau takes the brunt of a prejudice which results, it would seem, not entirely from a sense of moral indignation, but also from an unacknowledged sense of indebtedness as well as from a realization that Rousseau's independence represents an achievement that neither Keller nor Heinrich was ever able to attain. One must also take into account that Keller's opinion of Rousseau was probably deformed by the hostile views of Grimm and Diderot: "Das war ein einheitliches organisches Dasein [Schillers Leben]; Leben und Denken, Arbeit und Geist dieselbe Bewegung. Aber es gibt doch auch ein getrenntes, gewissermassen unorganisches Leben von gleicher Ehrlichkeit und Friedensfülle: das ist, wenn einer täglich ein bescheidenes dunkles Werk verrichtet, um die stille Sicherheit für ein freies Denken zu gewinnen, Spinoza, der optische Gläser schleift. Aber schon bei Rousseau, der Noten schreibt, verzerrt sich das gleiche Verhältnis ins Widerwärtige, da er weder Frieden noch Stille darin sucht, vielmehr sich wie die Andren quält, er mag sein, wo er will" (VI, 42).

58. Gusdorf concludes his essay on autobiography as follows: "Le privilège de l'autobiographie consiste donc, au bout du compte, en ce qu'elle nous montre non pas les étapes objectives d'une carrière, dont le relevé exact est la tâche de l'historien, mais bien l'effort d'un créateur pour donner le sens de sa propre légende," *op. cit.*, p. 123. This holds true for Rousseau, but not for Keller who, rather than giving meaning to this own legend, creates a legend to enable him ". . . noch einmal die alten grünen Pfade der Erinnerung zu wandeln" (VI, 325). It is worthwhile to contrast this ending of Keller's autobiographical novel—a novel *has* to end, *ought* to end, and therein lies one of the difficulties of the genre—with Rousseau's conclusion to his *Confessions*, which end in silence, inasmuch as an authentic autobiography cannot end, unless its author commits suicide, there being no illustrious example of such an occurrence.

59. Cf. Walter Hahn: Keller "betrachtet letzten Endes das Glück als eine Art Gnade, also als ein transzendentes Element, das vom Menschen nicht verdient, sondern einfach nur empfangen werden kann." "G. Kellers Auffassung des Glücks," *Proceedings Pacific Northwest Conference on Foreign Languages*, vol. XVII (Victoria, B.C., 1967), p. 151.

60. On this question of *Entsagung*, one may contrast the viewpoints of Theodor Storm and Georg Lukács. In a letter to Keller, dated April 30, 1881, Storm offers the following critique: "Ich habe Ihren 'Grünen Heinrich,' da ich zu Ende war, mit recht wehem Herzen fortgelegt, und ich sass noch lange, von dem Gefühl der Vergänglichkeit überschattet. Ihre liebsten Gestalten, der Grüne und Judith, Landolt und Figura Leu, lassen, wenn die späte Stunde des Glücks endlich da ist, die Arme hängen und stehen sich in schmerzlicher Resignation gegenüber, statt in resoluter Umarmung Vergangenheit und Gegenwart ans Herz zu schliessen. Das sind ganz lyrische, ich möchte sagen: biographische Ausgänge; und da hab ich mich gefragt: Ist das der Punkt, der Spalt, der jene 'befreienden' Spässe aufwirft? Sie brauchen mir nicht zu antworten." (Storm refers to the rowdy conclusion of *Die arme Baronin*). *Der Briefwechsel zwischen Theodor Storm und Gottfried Keller*, ed. Albert Köster (Berlin, 1904), p. 111. Lukács, referring specifically to Storm's theory that

Keller's *Entsagende* are erotic failures, counters it precisely with Keller's arguments concerning the disharmony of Rousseau's life (cf. footnote 59): "Die Kellersche Entsagung hängt vielmehr mit der tiefsten Problematik seiner ganzen Existenz zusammen, mit der Unmöglichkeit, künstlerische Tätigkeit und Leben, volles Auswirken der eigenen Persönlichkeit und nützliches staatsbürgerliches Wirken zu einer kompromisslosen, vollkommenen Einheit zu bringen." *Op. cit.*, p. 61. Lukács concludes: "Heinrichs Scheitern ist unmittelbar wirtschaftlich bedingt." *Ibid.*, p. 113. Furthermore, one may add that Settembrini, last great *Erzieher* within the genre of the *Bildungsroman*, defending an essentially liberal variety of Rousseauean theses, finds himself, and is found to be, in the dilemma of leading a disharmonious life—a dilemma not unlike the one which Keller assigns to Rousseau, and Lukács, alias Naphta, to Keller.

Footnotes to Chapter V

All quotations from Thoreau refer to the *Portable Thoreau*, ed. by Carl Bode (New York, 1959); quotations from Rousseau, unless stated otherwise, refer to his *Oeuvres complètes*, 4 vols., éd. Pléiade (1959–1969).

1. *Walden*, p. 259.
2. Walther Harding, *A Thoreau Handbook* (New York, 1959), p. 103. Cf. *The Saturday Review* (Edinburgh) Vol. 18 (December 3, 1864), p. 694, "An American Rousseau": "Mr. Henry David Thoreau appears to have been, in a mild unobstrusive way, a sort of American Rousseau." In a long chapter entitled "Rousseau en Amérique du Nord" in *Essais de littérature comparée* (Fribourg, 1964), François Jost bemoans the neglect of Rousseau on the part of American scholars. His own essay fails to mention this study—the first on Rousseau and Thoreau—which appeared in a slightly abbreviated version in *Yale French Studies*, Number 28, dedicated to Jean-Jacques Rousseau (Fall-Winter, 1961), pp. 112–120. Consult also Paul Merril Spurlin, *Rousseau in America 1760–1809* (University of Alabama Press, 1969).
3. *Ibid.*
4. Emerson, "Lecture on Transcendentalism" quoted by Pochman, *German Culture in America* (Madison, 1957), p. 79.
5. Frothingham, *Transcendentalism in New England* (New York, 1886), p. 144, quoted by Pochmann, *op. cit.*, p. 80.
6. *Ibid.*
7. Parker, *Works*, Cent. Ed. 15 vol. (Boston 1907–13), VI, p. 37, quoted by Pochmann, p. 80.
8. Pochmann, *op. cit.*, p. 432.
9. Hegel, *Phenomenology of Mind*, transl. Baillie (London, 1931), p. 598.
10. Temmer, *Time in Rousseau and Kant* (Geneva, 1958).
11. Coleridge, *Philosophical Lectures* (London, 1949), p. 308.
12. *Walden*, p. 272.
13. *Concord and Merrimack Rivers*, p. 210.
14. *Walden*, p. 272.
15. *Ibid.*, p. 349.
16. *Walking*, p. 628.
17. Unpublished doctoral dissertation, Yale University (1944).
18. *Walden*, p. 364.
19. Rousseau, *Correspondance* éd. T. Dufour (Paris, 1924–34), VII, p. 73 (lettre à Malesherbes).
20. *Walden*, p. 351.

21. *A Natural History of Massachusetts*, p. 34.
22. *Concord and Merrimack Rivers*, p. 195.
23. *A Natural History of Massachusetts*, p. 51.
24. *Concord and Merrimack Rivers*, p. 222.
25. *Walden*, p. 465.
26. *Ibid.*, p. 466.
27. *Essay on Civil Disobedience*, p. 111.
28. *Ibid.*, p. 109.
29. *Walden*, p. 420.
30. It is worthwhile to note that Herbert Marcuse's philosophy incorporates many ideas common to Rousseau and Thoreau—ideas which, to be sure, have been modified by Hegelian, Marxist and Freudian doctrines. Yet, the overall critique of contemporary Western civilization by Marcuse retains many features of Rousseau's and Thoreau's respective world views.
31. It should be added that Rousseau's life was richer than that of Thoreau, who seems to have known little of love. Rousseau, at least, believed in it—this being the sense of George Sand's quip: "Je lui pardonne tout puisqu'il a cru à l'amour."
32. *Journal*, quoted by Carl Bode in his introd., *op. cit.*, p. 27.
33. *Ibid.*, p. 233.
34. *Walden*, p. 386.
35. It is evident that my interpretation of Rousseau's quest for unity is relatively old-fashioned. Partially derived from my book (*op. cit.*) which in turn is based on theses by Kant, Hegel, Fichte, Lanson, Hazard, Cassirer, Hoeffding, Munteano, Peyre and Marcel Raymond, my views on Rousseau attempt to respect to the best of my ability the integrity of his art, thought, and life. I believe that they should not be twisted to conform to ideological structures of our age. Paul de Man's brilliant essay "The Rhetoric of Blindness: Jacques Derrida's Reading of Rousseau" in *Blindness and Insight* (New York, 1971) exemplifies my point of view.